A STRAIGHTFORWARD GUIDE TO TAXATION FOR SMALL TO MEDIUM SIZE BUSINESS

COLIN RICHARDS

Editor: Roger Sproston

Straightforward Publishing
www.straightforwardbooks.co.uk

Straightforward Guides

© Straightforward Co Ltd 2024

All rights reserved. No part of this publication may be reproduced in a retrieval system or transmitted by any means, electronic or mechanical, photocopying or otherwise, without the prior permission of the copyright holders.

ISBN

978-1-80236-299-2

Printed by 4edge www.4edge.co.uk

Cover design by BW Studio Derby

Whilst every effort has been made to ensure that the information contained within this book is correct at the time of going to press, the author and publisher can take no responsibility for the errors or omissions contained within.

Contents

Introduction and General Overview   13

Chapter 1-How the Tax System operates in the UK   21

How the tax system works	21
HMRC	21
Assessment of taxes-Self Assessment	22
Claiming tax relief	23
Registering for Self Assessment	23
Companies	24
Maintaining tax records	24
Cash basis accounting	25
When cash basis might not suit your business	25
Who can use cash basis	26
Who can't use the scheme	27
Keeping records	27
Inaccurate or late returns	27
HMRC compliance checks	28

Chapter 2--Choosing a Business Structure   29

The sole or proprietary business	29
Partnerships	30
Limited liability partnership (LLP)	31

The limited liability company	31
What type of business would suit me?	33
Notifying HMRC	33

Chapter 3-The Range of Taxes Businesses are Liable For 35

Direct taxes	35
Indirect taxes	36
Income tax	36
Calculation of personal Income Tax	38
Calculation of income tax for sole traders	38
Companies and Corporation Tax	38
The payment of dividends by a Limited Company	39
Capital gains tax	40
Capital Gains Tax allowances	41
Work out your total taxable gains	42
Tax rates from 6 April 2025	42
If you pay higher rate Income Tax	42
If you pay basic rate Income Tax	42
Inheritance tax	43
Inheritance Tax rates	44
Passing on a home	44
Giving away a home before you die	44
Gifts	45
Exempted gifts	46
The 7 year rule	47

Double-taxation treaties 48
National Insurance 48
National Insurance classes 49
Payment of National Insurance 49
VAT returns 50

Chapter 4-Calculating Profit and Loss of a Business 51

Calculation of profits 51
The preparation of accounts 51
Accounting conventions 52
Calculating income 53
Expenses 54
Direct expenses 55
Overheads 55
Capital and revenue expenditure 56
Drawings from a business if you are a sole trader or partner 56
Calculating profits 58
Profit averaging 59
Calculating losses 60
Sole traders or partnerships 60
Companies 61
Trading losses 61

*

Chapter 5-Business Equipment-Capital Allowances 63

General Allowances	63
Other capital allowances	63
What counts as plant and machinery	64
Integral features	65
Fixtures	65
If you let residential property	65
Annual investment allowance	65
What you can't claim on	66
When you can claim	66
If you don't want to claim the full cost	66
Items you also use outside your business	67
If you spend more than the AIA amount	67
Mixed partnerships	67
More than one business or trade	68
First year allowances	68
Business cars	69
Sole traders and partners	69
Employees	69
What counts as a car	69
What doesn't count	70
Rates for cars	70
Using cars outside your business	72
How to claim	73
When you can claim	73

Chapter 6. Giving to Charity — 75

Overview	75
Different rules for sole traders and partnerships.	75
Donating money	76
Payments that don't qualify	76
If you're given something in return	76
Equipment and trading stock	77
Giving equipment	77
Giving trading stock	77
VAT	78
Land, property and shares	78
What you get	79
Work out the market value	79
What you need to do	79
Land or property	79
Shares	80
Selling land, property or shares on behalf of a charity	80
Seconding employees	80
Sponsoring a charity	81
What qualifies	81
How to claim	81
Deduct from your profits	82
Deduct as business expenses	82
Claim capital allowances	82
If you donate more than your profit	82

Chapter 7-Paying for Employees	85
Taxes to pay when employing someone	85
Coronavirus eligibility	86
Statutory Maternity Pay and leave	86
Statutory Maternity Pay (SMP)	87
Statutory Paternity Pay and leave	88
Shared parental leave	88
Adoption pay	89
Company directors	88
Self-employed or a partner	89
Registering as an employer	89
Operating a payroll scheme	90
Taking on a new member of staff	92
Check you need to pay someone through PAYE	92
Working out if someone is an employee or self-employed	93
Temporary or agency workers	93
Employees you only pay once	93
Volunteers	94
Students	94
Get employee information	94
If your employee has more than one P45	95
Work out your employee's tax code	95
Student loan repayments	96
What you need to do	96

Special rules 97
Stopping deductions 97
Registering your new employee 97
Taxing Perks-benefits in kind 98

Chapter 8-Business Premises 105

Operating a business from home 105
Renting a business premises 106
Purchasing a business property 107
Freehold sales and transfers 108
New leasehold sales and transfers 108
How much you'll pay 109
Financing your property 109
Selling a business property 110
Capital allowances 110
Leases of property 111
Disposing of business property 111
Business Asset Disposal relief 112
Rollover relief 115
Eligibility 115
Partial relief 116
How to claim 116
SEED Enterprise Investment Scheme Relief 117

*

Chapter 9-Dealing With VAT	**119**
Charging VAT	119
Responsibilities	119
Making tax digital	120
VAT rates	122
Standard rate	122
Reduced rate	122
Zero rate	123
What you must do when charging VAT	123
VAT-inclusive and exclusive prices	124
When not to charge VAT	124
Exempt goods and services	125
VAT registration	125
Charging VAT to charities	126
Free goods and services	126
Providing services to EU businesses	126

Chapter 10-Business and Pensions	**129**
The State Pension	129
Occupational pensions	130
Private Pension Savings-General-The lifetime allowance	131
The annual allowance	132
Limits to benefits and contributions	132
Automatic enrolment	133

Choosing a pension scheme 137
Opt-out 138
Self-employed: what kind of pension should I use? 139

Chapter 11-Closing Down, Selling/Passing on a Business **143**

1. Closing a business down **143**
Self-employed or partnership-unincorporated business 143
Income tax 144
Allocating profits to tax years 144
Overlap relief 144
Treatment of stock 145
Treatment of capital allowances 145
Any income or expenses incurred after your business has ceased trading 146
PAYE scheme 146
VAT registration 146
Closing down a limited company 147
Striking a company off the register of companies 147
Deregistering for VAT 147
Closing down a PAYE scheme 148
Making staff redundant 149
2. Selling a business **150**
Sole traders 150
Partners 152
Limited company 152

11

VAT	153
Cash or shares?	153
Earn out	154
Other important areas to consider	154
3. Passing on a business	**155**
Giving away your business	155
Gifts relief	156
Eligibility	156
If you're giving away business assets	157
If you're giving away shares	147
Working out the relief	157
How to claim	157
Inheritance tax	158
If you die-what happens to your business?	158

Useful addresses and websites
Appendix 1. National Insurance Classes and Rates 2024/2025
Index

****

Introduction and General Overview

As the title suggests, this book, updated to 2024, deals with small to medium size businesses and taxation as it affects such businesses. Small businesses include sole traders and partnerships plus limited companies. The book doesn't deal with larger more complicated businesses such as Public Limited Companies, as accounts and taxes tend to be more complex and professional advice is needed (and usually employed).

Most of the areas covered in the introduction will be covered in more depth as we go through the book. As part of the overall approach, we will start by dealing with the range of taxes payable, including personal taxes, which are an integral part of the whole calculation when arriving at the final tax returns to HMRC. We then take a structured approach to outlining tax liabilities, detailing:

- the overall operation of the tax system in the United Kingdom.
- the actual process of forming a business within the framework of taxation.
- the calculation of profit and loss from a business.
- how to deal with calculation of business equipment from a tax standpoint.
- the all-important costs of employees; business premises; the dreaded VAT.
- closing down or selling a business.

With regard to VAT, we will outline the new liability for making a digital return for those registered for VAT.

First, before setting off, we should look at business generally, starting and running a business, the concepts of profit and loss, self assessment, the form of your business such as sole trader or limited company and what happens when you have built up a business and decide to either close it down or sell it on.

Tax and business generally

One of the main areas to think about at the outset is what type of business do you want? This is important because the type of business will have an impact on the taxes that you pay. You will need to decide whether you want to operate outside of the framework of a limited company and be a sole trader or partner or whether you want to set up a limited company. Basically, businesses can be Sole Traders, Partnerships, a Limited Company or a Limited Liability Partnership. What binds all business is the need to keep books of account and present final accounts to HMRC. Whether or not a company is more tax efficient depends very much on how profitable the business is and how much you intend to take from the business for your personal use.

Sole-Trader

This is a self-employed individual who is personally financially responsible if things go wrong, for example if the business cannot pay its debts and taxes. If problems occur, the individual's home and assets may be at risk.

A Partnership

This is more than one self-employed person working together to make a profit and sharing everything on an agreed split. Each partner is personally responsible for all debts run up by the partnership as a whole except for tax debts (individuals are responsible for their own tax debts).

A Limited Company

This is a separate legal structure where the liability of owners of the business is limited to the amount of their shares. Any legal action has to be against the company not the shareholders and the shareholders personal assets are safe.

A Limited Liability Partnership

This has many of the features of a normal partnership-but it is like a limited company in that members of an LLP cannot usually lose more than they invest.

Business accounts

Accounts are a summary of the business's financial activities for a period of time, commonly 12 months. Accounts can also be referred to as financial statements. A business will need accounts to see how the business is doing, to raise money for the business (bank managers will always want to see accounts), to raise money for the owners, i.e. for loans and mortgages, for insurance claims, for making tax returns, for partners in a partnership to see what is their share, for businesses which are a company for filing with Companies House and, finally, when it comes to sell the business, then the purchaser will want to see past and current accounts.

Using an accountant

You can either use an accountant or prepare your accounts yourself. This will depend on the type and complexity of your business. A bank or building society, or any other reputable lender loaning money will always, without exception want to see your final accounts prepared by an accountant, someone who is independent of the business. Many lenders will ask for copies of tax returns if the businessman is a sole trader or partnership as their tax returns show the accounts figures. This is provided the tax returns are prepared by a qualified accountant.

HM Revenue and Customs will expect profits of a business to be calculated in accordance with current accepted accountancy principles. HMRC are more likely to challenge a tax return received from a business if it was prepared without an accountant. HMRC have the power to charge tax for tax years going back up to 6 years and charge interest. All in all, it is very advisable to use an accountant, particularly if you are a limited company.

HMRC

Having decided what form your business should take you will then need to inform HMRC about your business activities. If you are self-employed or a partner, you will be registered to pay Class 2 National Insurance (see appendix for current NI rates). You should also consider registering for VAT, either compulsorily or voluntarily (see chapter 8 on VAT).

If you have employees, or if you are yourself receiving a salary you will need to set up a PAYE scheme. It is very important to stick rigorously to the regulations considering registration, as the penalties from HMRC for not keeping them informed and failing to pay what is due can be quite heavy. You can find out more about PAYE schemes by visiting hmrc.gov.uk.

When you consider starting up a business you are entitled to two important tax breaks:

- Pre-trading tax breaks-as the name suggest you can claim expenses incurred in the seven years run up to commencement of trading providing you retain receipts;
- Capital assets such as any equipment and vehicles owned by you in connection with the business before the business gets off the ground-these can be factored into the business at their market value.

Running your business

When your business is operative you will then have to be thinking about tax, as this is a major expense and should be budgeted for. If matters are simple and you are not registered for VAT and you employ no one then your main concern will be the tax bill at the end of each tax year.

However, as soon as you take on employee's or begin to pay directors then you will be in a position where you will need to deduct income tax and National Insurance contributions. In addition, it will be important to deduct Employer's Class 1 NI contributions which will be a cost on top of salary. Detailed PAYE records need to be kept and the tax deducted must be paid to HMRC each month.

The importance of recording profit and losses

The amount of tax you pay at the end of the accounting year is governed by what is the extent of your business profit or loss. The calculation of profit or loss for tax purposes is straightforward although the accounting conventions can be complex and are ever changing. To calculate profit or loss you should:

- Maintain accurate records of your income, outgoings and your bank transactions-it is important to maintain these records otherwise you will be subject to a hefty fine.
- You will need to choose an accounting date. If you are self-employed or a partner then this date might coincide with the end of the tax year- (April 6-April 5th). You can choose a different date in order to gain a cash-flow advantage in the short term but you still pay the same tax at the end.

- Draw up your final accounts based on the records that have been maintained. Small unincorporated businesses have the option of showing 'cash' accounts (see chapter 1) detailing just their business receipts and payments There is a requirement for larger businesses to prepare detailed accounts and to adjust them on a periodic basis in order to ensure compliance with tax law, for example taking into account finer points such as capital allowances and repairs and improvements.

If you are a sole trader or a partner in a business you will pay income tax and Class 4 NI contributions on your profits. Limited companies will pay corporation tax. Profits of a business are calculated before deducting the drawings of a proprietor, in the case of a sole trader or partner, or dividends in the case of a Limited company.

It goes without saying that if you make a loss you will not pay any tax. It may be possible to claim a refund of tax by setting the loss against any other income for the year or by carrying the loss forward to be offset against future profits, which will lessen the future tax burden.

Self-assessment
The current income and corporation tax system is known as self-assessment. We will look in more depth at self-assessment in Chapter 1. When you tell HMRC that you are a trading entity then you will need to fill in a tax return at the

end of the tax year (5th April) if you are either self-employed or a partner. If you are trading as a limited company, you will file your tax return at the end of your accounting period. For companies the deadline is 12 months after the end of the tax year and returns for sole traders and partners have to be filed either by 31st October for paper returns or online forms by January 31st the following year.

The tax return constitutes a self-assessment of your tax liability, with the final calculation forming the basis of your tax liability. Sole traders and partners usually pay income tax and Class 4 contributions twice a year on July 31st and January 31st each year. The due date for payment of tax if you are a limited company is nine months and one day after the end of the accounting period. Late filing or an inaccurate return will incur a penalty unless there is a cast-iron case for not filing or inaccuracies in the return. It goes without saying that HMRC have sweeping powers to check your records if they feel that there is a problem. They can visit your premises and go through the books with you-so be as thorough and transparent as possible!

****

Chapter 1

How the Tax System Operates in the UK

How the tax system works

In the introduction, I outlined generally the workings of the tax system. In this chapter we will look in more depth at the overall tax system and how it works in the UK.

In the United Kingdom, as in most other countries, the government raises taxes and spends these taxes in accordance with economic policies. Taxes can be levied by local authorities in addition to government. The UK tax year runs from 6th of April to 5th of April the following year. If you are self- employed then your accounting year does not have to run for the same period and you can select any date you want. Most people use the actual formal tax year because it is easier to administer.

Each year there is an annual budget, (plus Spring statements) delivered in Autumn, which is a statement of how things are in relation to the annual budget and the nations finances generally.

HMRC

HM Revenue and Customs (HMRC) are responsible for the collection of all taxes except for rates and council tax. HMRC also administers tax credits, the minimum wage, statutory sick pay, maternity pay, paternity and adoption pay and student loans. Therefore, HMRC has a wide remit.

Assessment of taxes-Self Assessment

Individuals are responsible for self-assessing their own tax and National Insurance liabilities and payments of any loans. This is achieved by filling in an annual tax return. Individuals are usually notified that they must complete a tax return. The return can either be sent by post or more likely online-the dates being 31st October for paper returns and 31st January for online filing.

you must send a tax return if, in the last tax year (6 April to 5 April), any of the following applied:

- you were self-employed as a 'sole trader' and earned more than £1,000 (before taking off anything you can claim tax relief on).
- you were a partner in a business partnership.
- you had a total taxable income of more than £100,000.
- you had to pay Capital Gains Tax when you sold or 'disposed of' something that increased in value.
- you had to pay the High Income Child Benefit Charge.
- You may also need to send a tax return if you have any untaxed income, such as:
- some COVID-19 grant or support payments.
- money from renting out a property.
- tips and commission.

- income from savings, investments and dividends.
- foreign income.

For more detailed information go to:
www.gov.uk/self-assessment-tax-returns/sending-return

If you've been told to send a return

If you get an email or letter from HM Revenue and Customs telling you to send a return, you must send it - even if you don't have any tax to pay. If you used to send a tax return but don't need to send one for the last tax year, you can contact HMRC to close your Self- Assessment account. You must also tell HMRC if you've stopped being self-employed.

Claiming tax relief

Fill in a tax return to claim money back from HMRC for:
- Donations to charity.
- private pension contributions as a higher or additional rate taxpayer, or if your scheme isn't set up for automatic tax relief.
- work expenses over £2,500.

Registering for self-assessment

If you've never submitted a return before, you will first need to register for Self Assessment. There are different ways to register if you're self-employed, not self-employed but need to declare income, or if you're in a partnership. The government website www.gov.uk/log-in-file-self-assessment-tax-return will guide you. If you're new to Self-Assessment, you'll need to keep records (for example bank statements or receipts) so you can fill in your tax return correctly.

Companies

For limited companies, the period covered by your return will be your accounting period as opposed to the tax year. So if your tax year runs from 1st November to October 30th your tax return will run from this date. The corporation tax return must be filed within 12 months of the end of the company's tax period. All company forms must be filed electronically. All employers are required to provide details of National Insurance and other deductions that they take from employees, each time they run a payroll. This is called Real Time Information. For details of this and the relevant other statutory returns see chapter 6 on paying for employees.

Maintaining tax records

Most people who are required to keep accounts will use a software package to assist them. There is no rule saying you have to do this; accounts can also be handwritten as long as they are understandable. A common way is to record the information on a spreadsheet. As a minimum requirement, you will need to achieve the following:

- Record income-this can be daily or weekly as long as it is accurately recorded. You need to retain till rolls, copies

of any invoices and also appointment books and any work diaries.
- Record sums paid into your business bank account. You will need to keep all bank statements and paying-in books to be able to identify all transactions through your account.

In addition to this information, you need an accurate record of your debtors and also creditors. The value of your stock needs to be accurately maintained and any work in hand such as uncompleted work. Cash on hand needs to be accounted for and also any equipment and assets within your business. Some records and adjustments are not necessary if you prepare your accounts on a cash basis.

Cash basis accounting

'Cash basis' is a way to work out your income and expenses for your self-assessment tax return, if you're a sole trader or partner. If you run a small business, cash basis accounting may suit you better than traditional accounting. This is because you only need to declare money when it comes in and out of your business.

At the end of the tax year, you won't have to pay Income Tax on money you didn't receive in your accounting period.

When cash basis might not suit your business

Cash basis probably won't suit you if you:

- want to claim interest or bank charges of more than £500 as an expense.
- run a business that's more complex, eg you have high levels of stock.
- need to get finance for your business - a bank could ask to see accounts drawn up using traditional accounting to see what you owe and are due before agreeing a loan.
- have losses that you want to offset against other taxable income ('sideways loss relief').

Who can use cash basis

You can use cash basis if you:

- run a small self-employed business, eg sole trader or partnership.
- have an income of £150,000 or less a year.

If you have more than one business, you must use cash basis for all your businesses. The combined turnover from your businesses must be less than £150,000.

If you use cash basis and your business grows during the tax year

You can stay in the scheme up to a total business income of £300,000 per year. Above that, you'll need to use traditional accounting for your next tax return.

Who can't use the scheme

Limited companies and limited liability partnerships can't use cash basis. There are also some specific types of businesses that can't use the scheme, for more details go to www.gov.uk/simpler-income-tax-cash-basis/who-can-use-cash-basis. If you can't use cash basis, you'll need to use traditional accounting to work out your taxable profits. With regards to your personal tax return, you will need to keep records of interest paid, pensions received, benefits received, pension contributions, gifts to charities and any capital gains.

Keeping records

If you are self-employed you need to keep your records for five years and ten months from the end of the tax year. For limited companies you are required to maintain records for 6 years. PAYE and CIS (Construction Industry records) must be kept for three years in addition to the current tax year. If you fail to keep these records then you can be fined by HMRC.

Companies must complete an annual return form (CT600) and file it online, together with accounts and tax computations. HMRC can advise on completion. You should go to their website www.hmrc.gov/ukct/managing/company-tax-return/index.htm.

Inaccurate or late returns

If you make an honest error, you can correct this as you go, or later by following a set procedure. However, if you file an inaccurate return deliberately or carelessly you can be fined. If you have filed your return late you will receive automatic penalties. The scale of the penalty will depend on the lateness of the return. Details of fines can be found on the HMRC website.

HMRC compliance checks

HMRC can check all supporting documents and will do so if they believe that there is a problem with tax return information. They will also randomly check tax returns. HMRC will give you notice of an enquiry. You can appeal against the outcome of a compliance check.

****

Chapter 2

The Process of Starting a Business-Choosing a Structure

As we saw in the introduction, there are various structures within which your business can operate and it is essential, when formulating your business plan that you understand the nature of each structure.

The sole or proprietary business

This is a business owned by one person. If you are operating alone then this may be suitable for your purposes. The person and the business are legally one and the same. It does not matter what or who you trade as, the business is inseparable from yourself, as opposed to a limited company, which is a separate entity. All financial risk is taken by that one person and all that person's assets are included in that risk. The one big advantage is that all decisions can be taken by the one person without interference.

A second advantage is that the administrative costs of running a sole business are small. If your business is VAT registered then you will need to keep records, as you will for Her Majesty's Revenue and Customs. However, there are no other legal requirements.

Partnerships

Partnership is a business where two or more people are joined by an agreement to run that business together. The agreement is usually written, (given the potential pitfalls that can arise from a partnership).

Liabilities which may arise are shared jointly and severally and this should be made clear to anyone entering a partnership. Even if you only have 1% of the business you will still be responsible for 100% of the liability. All personal assets of each partner are at risk if the business fails.

Decisions are taken jointly, as laid down by the partnership agreement. If the agreement lays down that partners have differing decision-making capacity dependent upon their shareholding, then it could be that, in a three-way partnership, the decision making process may be hampered because a decision cannot be reached unless the major investor is present.

It is very important indeed to consider the nature of the agreement that you are entering into and it may also be advisable to take legal advice. Partnership usually reflects the way that business was capitalised although other factors may be taken into consideration. For example, an expert in a particular field may join with an investor to create a 50/50 partnership.

It is very advisable indeed to carefully consider the ramifications of entering a partnership. Many such arrangements end in tears, with both partners hostile to each other. Personal bankruptcy can occur as can the ruin of the partner(s). Profits are usually shared between partners in accordance with the terms in the agreement.

Limited liability partnership (LLP)

Limited liability partnerships combine some features of a limited company and some of a partnership. Like a company, the members of an LLP are not personally liable for business debts. Provided that they are not negligent, individual partners risk only their partnership investment. The income tax treatment of an LLP is the same as an ordinary partnership. Profits are shared out between members in accordance with the partnership agreement. Each member is taxed as if they were running their own self-employed business paying Class 2 NI contributions and income tax and Class 4 NI on trading profits. The LLP is also responsible for setting up a PAYE system and VAT registration.

The Limited Liability Company

This type of company has evolved over the years and provides a framework within which a business can operate effectively. A limited company is usually the best vehicle for business, in all but the smallest of business. It is certainly the only sensible answer if capital is being introduced by those who are not actively involved in running the business (shareholders).

Shareholders inject capital and receive a return (dividend) in proportion to the capital they invest. They are eligible to attend an Annual General Meeting to approve or otherwise the way the directors are running the business. Annual General Meetings also determine how much of the profit will be distributed to shareholders.

Voting is in accordance with the number of shares held and the meeting can replace all or any of the directors if a majority are dissatisfied with them. Shareholders can, if a majority request, call an Extraordinary General Meeting to question directors about performance, outside the cycle of Annual General Meetings. Control of the company is in the hands of directors who are appointed by the shareholders to run the company on their behalf.

The company is a legal entity in its own right and stands alone from the directors and shareholders, who have limited liability.

When a company is created it will have an "Authorised Shareholding" that specifies the limit of a shareholders liability. If all shares have been issued then shareholders are not liable for any more debts that the company may accrue.

As mentioned, the biggest single advantage of a Limited Company is that you are not personally liable for any business debts. Whilst you will lose business assets and your shares will be worthless, your personal property is protected unless it is pledged to a bank to secure a loan or overdraft.

As a company director, you are an employee of the company and have to pay income tax and national insurance on a salary. You can also take dividends and will pay tax at the current rate.

What type of business would suit me?

Whether you operate as a limited company, partner or sole trader depends on a number of factors, including:

- How much profit the business makes.
- How much money you need for your personal use.
- The amount you need to invest in the business.
- The liability to others.
- The scope to pay significant dividends.

You would need to see an accountant who will help you make the necessary calculations to help you make a decision. Bear in mind the following:

- Running a company is more complicated than being self-employed.
- Forming a company is relatively straightforward-getting rid of one is not so straightforward.

Notifying HMRC

Whichever route you take, Sole trader, partner, limited company, when you set up a business you need to notify HMRC of:

- The effective trading date.
- Taking on employees (see chapter 6 on employees).
- Registering for VAT (see chapter 7 on VAT).

There is an automatic fine if you fail to do so. To register you should visit the HMRC website at https://www.gov.uk/new-business-register-for-tax. You can also register as a sole trader at https://www.gov.uk/set-up-sole-trader.

In the next chapter, we will discuss tax liability for business which should give you an idea of the various liabilities faced by sole traders and limited companies.

****

Chapter 3

The Range of Taxes Businesses Are Liable For

Having considered the operation of the tax system and the process of starting a business, we need to move on to understanding the range of taxes that businesses are responsible for so that you have a clear picture of your potential liabilities.

You will find that there are two (main) types of taxes raised in the UK, direct taxes and indirect taxes. Income will be taxed directly along with profits and any capital gains. **Direct taxes** can be grouped into four categories:

- Income tax.
- Inheritance tax paid by the individual.
- Corporation tax paid by companies.
- Capital gains tax paid by both individuals and companies.

In addition to taxes there will be liability for National Insurance. All employers will be liable for Class 1 employer's contributions based on the wages and salary paid to employees including directors.

Indirect taxes are those taxes charged on items of expenditure and include VAT, other excise duties and any stamp duties in addition to industry specific taxes such as power generation, transport and banking.

HM Revenue and Customs are responsible for collection and repayment of taxes. Local authorities will collect other taxes such as council tax and business rates.

In summary:

Income tax is a tax paid by individuals and is charged on the following wide range of activities:
- Sole traders and partners engaged in business.
- All earnings from employment including salaries, wages, any perks taken from the company, any tips given, maternity pay, ordinary and additional paternity pay and adoption pay.
- Pensions, including the state pension and any private pensions.
- Some (but not all) benefits received from the state such as jobseeker's allowance, income support and employment and support allowance. Some recipients of child benefit, based on income being over £50,000 will also be taxed. (For full details of which benefits are taxable you should visit the Department of Work and Pensions-website.

- .www.gov.uk/organisations/department-for-work-pensions.
- Income from property, savings and investments and any other miscellaneous income such as trusts and any other casual income.

As you can see, income tax applies to most forms of income, few areas escape it, but there are certain types of income which are not liable for tax, including:
- Redundancy payments and other payments received when a job is lost.
- An element of pension lump sums (25%) on retirement or before if taken early.
- Some welfare benefits.
- Individual savings Accounts (ISA's).
- Premium bond income.
- Tax credits.

Income tax is payable on all income, by everyone living in the UK, whether or not it is earned here or abroad. If you are resident abroad you are still liable for UK tax on UK income. However, different rules may apply according to your residential status, for example those who are not ordinarily resident in the UK and it would be necessary to obtain professional advice as tax matters will inevitably be more complicated.

Calculation of personal Income Tax

When calculating personal income tax (as opposed to Corporation tax which is discussed below) you need to add all of your sources of income together to arrive at the total for the year. You will need to know the tax rates and your personal allowances for the particular year. You will find Tax rates and allowances for 2024/25 in appendix one.

Calculation of income tax for sole traders

There are a number of steps to follow when working out your liability for tax if you are a **sole trader**, as follows:

Deduct your personal allowance from your income-everyone has a personal allowance which increases each year-for 2024/2025 it is £12.570. It may be bigger if you claim marriage allowance or blind person's allowance. If your income in 2024/25 exceeds £100,000 then your allowances will be restricted. Basically, for every £2 over £100,000 your personal allowance goes down by £1. There is no personal allowance if taxable income is over £125,140. After you have deducted your personal allowance the first tranche of your income will be taxed at the basic rate of 20% from thereon the rates are as set out in appendix one.

Companies and Corporation Tax

As explained, the tax situation for limited companies is somewhat different to that of self-employed. Corporation tax is a tax paid by companies on their profits, and also any capital gains, during the financial year. The profits of a company will take into account all sources of income, including income from any investments and also from property, such as rents. As we shall see, there are differences in the way company profits are calculated, to those of a sole trader and partners. For example, companies, but not sole traders or partners can claim a tax deduction for expenditure on goodwill and intangible assets and other allowances, such as research and development, depending on their trade. If a company is a member of a group of companies, it is taxed on its own profits but groups are treated differently from individual companies in certain respects, including treatment of losses. For certain, if you are operating a group of companies, you will need specialist accounting.

Essentially, Corporation Tax is charged on the profits of all UK resident companies and also non-resident companies that trade in the UK through agencies or branches. Currently, Corporation tax is 25% (2024/25).

The payment of Dividends by a Limited Company
If your company pays a dividend, there is no tax to pay on that dividend but the dividend is not a tax-deductible expense in calculating your corporation tax bill. Dividends are paid with a 10% tax credit and unless the recipient is a higher or additional rate taxpayer there is no further income tax to pay on the dividend. Dividends are also not liable to National

Insurance. Dividends which the company receives are not liable to corporation tax.

Capital gains tax

Capital Gains Tax is a tax paid by individuals (sole traders and partners) and by companies on the profit when you sell (or 'dispose of') something (an 'asset') that's increased in value. It's the gain you make that's taxed, not the amount of money you receive. Some assets are tax-free. You also don't have to pay Capital Gains Tax if all your gains in a year are under your tax-free allowance.

Disposing of an asset includes:
- selling it.
- giving it away as a gift, or transferring it to someone else.
- swapping it for something else.
- getting compensation for it - like an insurance payout if it's been lost or destroyed.
- You pay Capital Gains Tax on the gain when you sell (or 'dispose of'):
- most personal possessions worth £6,000 or more, apart from your car.
- property that isn't your main home.
- your main home if you've let it out, used it for business or it's very large.
- shares that aren't in an ISA or PEP.
- business assets

These are known as 'chargeable assets'. Depending on the asset, you may be able to reduce any tax you pay by claiming a relief. If you dispose of an asset you own jointly with someone else, you have to pay Capital Gains Tax on your share of the gain. You don't usually pay tax on gifts to your husband, wife, civil partner or a charity. You don't pay Capital Gains Tax on certain assets, including any gains you make from:

- ISAs or PEPs.
- UK government gilts and Premium Bonds.
- Betting, lottery or pools winnings.
- Transactions between spouses and partners.
- Cars and other machinery and assets with a useful life of less than 50 years (but not where capital allowances have been claimed).
- Shares in Enerprise Schemes or SEED enterpise if held for at least three years.
- The disposal by a trading company of a substantial shareholding (10% plus) in another.
- Personal items sold for less than £6,000.
- Assets passed on death.
- Most life insurance proceeds.

Capital Gains Tax allowances

You only have to pay Capital Gains Tax on your overall gains above your tax-free allowance (called the Annual Exempt Amount). The tax-free allowance is (2024/25):

- £6,000
- £3,000 for trusts

Work out your total taxable gains
1. Work out the gain for each asset (or your share of an asset if it's jointly owned). Do this for the personal possessions, shares, property or business assets you've disposed of in the tax year.
2. Add together the gains from each asset.
3. Deduct any allowable losses.

You pay a different rate of tax on gains from residential property than you do on other assets. You don't usually pay tax when you sell your home.

If you pay higher rate Income Tax
If you're a higher or additional rate taxpayer, you'll pay:
- 28% on your gains from residential property
- 20% on your gains from other chargeable assets

If you pay basic rate Income Tax
If you're a basic rate taxpayer, the rate you pay depends on the size of your gain, your taxable income and whether your gain is from residential property or other assets.

1. Work out how much taxable income you have - this is your income minus your Personal Allowance and any other Income Tax reliefs you're entitled to.

2. Work out your total taxable gains.
3. Deduct your tax-free allowance from your total taxable gains.
4. Add this amount to your taxable income.
5. If this amount is within the basic Income Tax band you'll pay 10% on your gains (or 18% on residential property). You'll pay 20% (or 28% on residential property) on any amount above this.

For individuals, capital gains tax is paid through the self-assessment system. For companies, it is paid as part of the corporation tax bill.

Inheritance tax
Inheritance tax is paid on the capital value of your assets when you die and is paid to HMRC by the executors of your estate when you die. It can also be charged on some transactions during your life, such as gifts made within seven years of your death. However, companies are not liable for inheritance tax only individuals. Inheritance Tax is a tax on the estate (the property, money and possessions) of someone who's died.

There's normally no Inheritance Tax to pay if:
- the value of your estate is below the £325,000 threshold.
- you leave everything to your spouse or civil partner, a charity or a community amateur sports club

If you're married or in a civil partnership and your estate is worth less than £325,000, you can transfer any unused threshold to your partner when you die. This means their threshold can be as much as £650,000.

Inheritance Tax rates

Inheritance Tax is charged on your estate at 40%. The estate can pay Inheritance Tax at a reduced rate of 36% on some assets if you leave 10% or more of the 'net value' to charity in your will. If Inheritance Tax on gifts is due, it's charged on a sliding scale known as taper relief. Inheritance Tax reliefs, eg Business Relief, allow some assets to be passed on free of Inheritance Tax or with a reduced bill.

Passing on a Home

You can pass a home to your husband, wife or civil partner when you die. There's no Inheritance Tax to pay if you do this. If you leave the home to another person in your will, it counts towards the value of the estate. From 6 April 2017, new rules mean that a person gets a bigger Inheritance Tax threshold if they give away their main home to children (including adopted, foster or stepchildren) or grandchildren.

Giving away a home before you die: There's normally no Inheritance Tax to pay if you move out and live for another 7 years. If you want to continue living in your property after giving it away, you'll need to:

- pay rent to the new owner at the going rate (for similar local rental properties).
- pay your share of the bills.
- live there for at least 7 years.
- You don't have to pay rent to the new owners if the following apply:
- you only give away part of your property.
- the new owners also live at the property.
- If you die within 7 years.

If you die within 7 years of giving away all or part of your property, your home will be treated as a gift and the 7 year rule applies.

Gifts

There's usually no Inheritance Tax to pay on small gifts you make out of your normal income, eg Christmas or birthday presents. These are known as 'exempted gifts'. There's also no Inheritance Tax to pay on gifts between spouses or civil partners. You can give them as much as you like during your lifetime - as long as they live in the UK permanently.

Other gifts count towards the value of your estate. There may be Inheritance Tax to pay if you've given away more than £325,000, but only if you die within 7 years. Inheritance Tax on gifts is paid by the person who received the gift (the 'beneficiary') - not the estate.

What counts as a gift?

A gift can be:

- anything that has value, e.g. money, property, possessions.
- a loss in value when something's transferred, eg if you sell your house to your child for less than it's worth, the difference in value counts as a gift.

Exempted gifts

You can give away £3,000 worth of gifts each tax year (6 April to 5 April) without them being added to the value of your estate. This is known as your 'annual exemption'. You can carry any unused annual exemption forward to the next year - but only for one year.

Each tax year, you can also give away:

- wedding or civil ceremony gifts of up to £1,000 per person (£2,500 for a grandchild or great grandchild, £5,000 for a child).
- normal gifts out of your income, e.g. for Christmas or birthday presents - you must still be able to maintain your standard of living after making the gift.
- payments to help with another person's living costs, e.g. .an elderly relative or a child under 18.
- gifts to charities and political parties.

- You can use more than one of these exemptions on the same person, eg you could give your grandchild gifts for his/her birthday and wedding in the same tax year.
- Small gifts up to £250.
- You can give as many gifts of up to £250 per person as you want during the tax year as long as you haven't used another exemption on the same person.

The 7 year rule

If there's Inheritance Tax to pay, it's charged at 40% on gifts given in the 3 years before you die. Gifts made 3 to 7 years before your death are taxed on a sliding scale known as 'taper relief'.

Years between gift and death	Tax paid
less than 3	40%
3 to 4	32%
4 to 5	24%
5 to 6	16%
6 to 7	8%
7 or more	0%

Gifts are not counted towards the value of your estate after 7 years.

If your permanent home ('domicile') is abroad, Inheritance Tax is only paid on your UK assets, eg property or bank accounts you have in the UK. It's not paid on 'excluded assets' like:

- foreign currency accounts with a bank or the Post Office.
- overseas pensions.
- holdings in authorised unit trusts and open-ended investment companies.
- There are different rules if you have assets in a trust or government gilts, or you're a member of visiting armed forces.

When you won't count as living abroad

HMRC will treat you as being domiciled in the UK if you either:
- lived in the UK for 17 of the last 20 years.
- had your permanent home in the UK at any time in the last 3 years of your life.

Double-taxation treaties

Your executor might be able to reclaim tax through a double-taxation treaty if Inheritance Tax is charged on the same assets by the UK and the country where you lived.

NATIONAL INSURANCE

You will pay National Insurance (NI) if you are self-employed, employed, a partner, employer and by all who wish to protect their contributions so that they receive full state pension. Young people under 16 do not have to pay NI and those in full time education between 16-18 also do not have to pay as they are credited with contributions during that period. If you do not work because you are looking after children or severely disabled relatives for more than 20 hours per week, you will be entitled to a weekly credit.

National Insurance classes
The class you pay depends on your employment status and how much you earn, and whether you have any gaps in your National Insurance record. See appendix 1 for a summary of current (2024/25) NI classes and costs.

Payment of National Insurance
Class 1 National Insurance is collected through PAYE. Class 2 and 3 contributions are paid by monthly direct debit to the National Insurance Contributions Office (NICO) part of HMRC. Class 4 is collected through the self-assessment tax return as part of the sole traders or partners tax bill.

If you are self-employed or a partner you can claim small earnings exemption, which exempts you from paying Class 2 contributions if you expect your trading profits to fall below a certain threshold.

If you are both self-employed and employed in the same year you may pay Class 1 NI on your employed income and Class 4 contributions on your self-employed income. The amounts paid by you may be capped, as there is a maximum annual limit on the amounts to be paid. Irrespective of the number of self-employments you have you need only pay one lot of Class 2 contributions. Different amounts apply to Class 4 contributions.

Here, the profits from all of your self-employments must be added together to calculate your liability. For clarification on self employed and NI rates you should go to: www.gov.uk/self-employed-national-insurance-rates

VAT returns

VAT returns usually cover 3 months and have to be filed by the end of the 4th month. There are penalties or surcharges for late VAT returns. Penalties can be 2%, 5%, 10%, and 15% of the VAT due depending on how many returns have been late in a row. It is usually the case that HMRC write to businesses the first time that the return is late and only charge surcharges for future returns submitted late.

****

Chapter 4

Calculating Profit and Loss from a Business

In the previous chapters, we have looked at business and taxation generally. In this and subsequent chapters we will look more closely at business accounting.

Calculation of profits

One major area of confusion for anyone entering business for the first time (or anytime for that matter) is how taxable profits from a business, whether sole trader, partnership, or limited company, are calculated and what expenses are allowable.

Many sole traders use 5th of April as their year end as it is the end of the tax year and keeps matters simple. You can also use the date of 31st March as HMRC will treat this date as if it is 5th of April. If you choose 31st of March as the end of your tax year, your tax return would show your income and expenditure for the period 1st April to 31st March and if you choose 5th of April your returns would show income and expenditure from 6th April to 5th of April.

The preparation of accounts

Once you have selected a suitable year-end you then need to understand how to prepare accounts from the records that you have maintained for tax purposes. The first thing that you need to do is to prepare a trading profit and loss account which, essentially, summarises your income and expenditure for the accounting period. It is worth noting that most businesses also prepare a balance sheet which sets out the business's assets, liabilities and capital at the end of the year. These final accounts are then used to prepare your tax return.

Accounting conventions

Accounts for all businesses are prepared in accordance with what are known as Generally Accepted Accounting Principles (GAAP). These specific rules dictate that accounts must show at the year-end:

- Any debtors and creditors (people owing you money or money that you owe).
- Stocks of material or goods and work in progress which is valued according to set criteria.
- All your income, even on uncompleted contracts
- Liabilities only when they become due.

As we have discussed, some small, unincorporated businesses, particularly those without an accountant or with sales less than the VAT threshold, choose to prepare their accounts on a cash basis. Cash accounts are much simpler to prepare and work by adding up the income received by your business and deducting payments made for allowable expenses. This means that you do not have to include, or understand, debtors, creditors, stock, or work in progress, as these areas of accounting may not be applicable for your business. There is a threshold, currently £150,000 under which you can use the cash-accounting basis. For further details you should go to the HMRC website which provides more detailed advice.

Calculating income

If you are preparing accounts that comply with GAAP, then calculating your income is the first step in working out your trading profits. Income means the money that you have earned from selling goods and services in the trading period. If you run a business where you take cash or payment via card then the calculation is uncomplicated. It is where you run a business where people do not pay you straight away, where you invoice, that the accounting becomes more complex. You must adjust your sales receipts for opening and closing debtors. You add your closing debtors to your sales figures and deduct your opening debtors from it.

If you supply services over a period, you need to include a proportion of this income even if you do not invoice your client until after the end of your year-end. It is here that confusion can arise. .

Your turnover will exclude any interest received on a business bank account and rental income and profits that you may have made from selling assets, all of which will be listed separately on your tax return.

Expenses

After calculating your income, it is now time to look at the various deductions that can be claimed. There are two main types of expenses, direct expenses or what is known as the cost of sales and overheads. In addition, if you have equipment, you can claim capital allowances (see chapter 5).

Direct expenses

Direct expenses are, quite simply, those costs incurred when you sell your products or services. These costs will vary depending on the type of business that you run. An example of these costs might be:

- A tradesman, such as a carpenter or plumber, will have as direct costs materials and tools.
- Someone driving for a living, such as a taxi driver or delivery driver would have fuel and oil etc.
- A newsagent would have costs of stock.

Other businesses tend to be more complex. However, the common denominator is what you must buy to sell and make a profit. Direct costs are always tax deductible and must be adjusted for opening and closing stock and work in progress. Depreciation of plant and equipment are not allowed for tax purposes but capital allowances (see chapter 5) can be claimed.

Overheads

Most businesses incur overhead costs and they consist of administrative costs associated with selling goods or services. They are tax deductible as long as they are incurred exclusively for business purposes. Below is a list of typical overhead costs.

- Wages and salaries and any other costs of employment.
- Vehicle and travel expenses-these include all costs except for fines and penalties-travel from home to work is not allowable and also the cost of the vehicle is not allowed as this comes under capital expenditure. Travel by rail, air and taxi is tax deductible as is the cost of staying in hotels.
- Rent, rates and power plus insurance costs.
- Repairs and renewals of property and equipment but not the costs of renovation or improvement
- Telephone, stationary and other office costs.
- Advertising and business entertaining costs (within limits)
- Interest on bank and other loans but not capital repayments.
- Bank, credit card, and other finance charges.
- Irrecoverable debts written off.

- Accountancy, legal and other professional charges are all tax allowable, but there are some exceptions, such as the legal costs of buying plant and machinery as they are treated as part of the asset.
- Depreciation and profit or loss on the sale of assets- depreciation is where the item is written off over the useful life.
- Any other associated business expenses although there are restrictions, such as donations to charity and to political parties.

Capital and revenue expenditure

As we have discussed, capital expenditure is not tax deductible, but you can claim capital allowances. However, most revenue expenses are deductible. It can sometimes be difficult differentiating between capital and revenue expenditure. Basically, capital expenditure is fixed and permanent whilst revenue is fluid. For example, interest on bank charges and other finance costs (as we have seen) is tax deductible but not the loan itself, which is a capital item. Another example is repairs to a building or machinery are revenue costs- but the property or asset is capital and therefore not deductible.

Drawings from a business if a sole trader or partner

Sums that a sole trader or partner take from the business for their own personal expenditure are called 'drawings'. These items, or wages, are not a tax-deductible expense of the business as they amount to withdrawal of profits.

These payments can be in a number of forms:

- Regular payments by cash, cheque or standing order.
- Payment of personal bills from the business bank account.
- Tax and class 4 National Insurance payments
- Class 2 NI.
- Pension contributions.

Goods and services taken from a business for personal use

If goods are taken from a business for personal use, then taxable profits must be increased to take into account market value (not cost) of these goods. Likewise, the same principle applies if a benefit is gained by supplying services to a business owner.

Stock and work in progress

Accounts must include an adjustment for opening and closing stock and work in progress valued according to set rules. At the accounting year-end, stocks of unsold goods, parts and components must be valued at the lower of their cost or their selling price. Service businesses must include the value of any uncompleted contracts.

VAT

If you are not VAT registered, your expenses include VAT and the cost is tax-deductible. If you are VAT registered you will include VAT on most of your expenses on your VAT return.

Companies

Companies will deduct expenses in a similar way to sole traders and partners, although there are notable differences, mainly that expenses cannot be incurred for both business and private purposes, interest and bad debts which do not relate to the trade have to be accounted for under what is known as the 'loan relationship' rules. Companies can also claim tax relief on goodwill and tax credits on research and development and to clean up contaminated land.

Calculating profits

If you prepare cash accounts, you are quite simply taxed on your profit that is calculated as your receipts minus payments. However, if you prepare GAAP accounts, you pay tax on your profits as follows:

- Income; less
- Deductible expenses (direct costs and overheads); less
- Capital allowances.

If you make a profit from your business, there may be a further adjustment as follows:

- Profits can be apportioned between tax years, depending on your choice of year-end date.
- The profits can be averaged over more than one tax year (see below).
- Profits can be subject to special treatment.

Profit averaging

Certain groups, such as authors, farmers and artists often experience fluctuating profits, basically some years they might earn more than others due to what is produced. These groups are allowed to average their profits over consecutive tax years. Profits for these purposes are calculated after deducting capital allowances but before loss relief (see further on). Averaging relief can be claimed by sole traders and partners but not if you trade through a limited company. It cannot be claimed in the year in which a trade commences or ceases.

Profit averaging applies if:
- the profits of the lower year are less than 75% of the profits of the higher year; or
- the profits for one (but not both) tax years are nil.

If the profits for one of the years are more than 70% but less than 75% of the profits for the other year, the profit for each year is calculated according to a set formula. The result of the calculation is added to the profit of the lower year and deducted from the profit of the higher year.

You should note, in the accounting of income and expenditure that there are special rules for foster and other carers. You can obtain further information from www.gov.uk or from www.fostertax.co.uk/.

Calculating losses

It is a reality of business life that losses will occur, particularly in the first years of trading. Losses occur, on a simple level, when expenditure exceeds income. There are also other circumstances in which losses will occur which we will outline.

Sole traders and partnerships

When losses are made by sole traders or a partnership, tax relief can be claimed for the loss in various ways, depending on when and how the loss occurred, either in the early years of business, when the business stops trading or during trading.

There are various ways to offset losses:
- You can claim losses against other income received by the business, either in the year of the loss or the previous year.
- Claim against any capital gains.
- You can carry forward losses against any future profits
- Losses that occur in the first four years of a business can be set against income from the previous three tax years.

- Losses occurring in the 12 months to the date a business ceases trading can be claimed in the tax year when the business stops and the three previous tax years.

Companies

Companies are treated differently for tax purposes when making a loss. Sometimes companies deliberately create losses by paying directors bonuses or paying money into pension schemes. Sometimes, capital losses are made by selling an item below the cost at which it was bought.

Trading losses

Companies will claim tax relief for their losses in broadly the same way as individuals. They are either deducted from other profits and gains in the same accounting period. Any remaining balance can be carried back and offset against the profits of the previous year, carried forward to be used against future profits or used when a company ceases to trade. A loss arising in the last 12 months of a company trading can be carried back against the company's profits for the previous three years, using the later years first.

Capital losses

Capital losses occur if you sell capital assets for less than you bought them for. They can be deducted from the company's capital gains for the same accounting period or carried forward. They can't be carried back against previous accounting periods except in a few circumstances.

Loss claims for failed business investments

An individual (but not a company) can claim tax relief if they invest in shares in an unlisted company that fails. If the shares are rendered worthless, a capital gains tax loss is calculated in the usual way, but instead of deducting the loss from a capital gain it is deducted from your income. In order to make this loss, it is not necessary to sell the shares. Instead, under what are known as 'negligible value' rules the shares are treated as if you sold them to yourself at the current market value, i.e. at no value. You must make the claim in the year that you made the loss or the previous year. There are deadlines for making the claim. It must be made in writing on or before the second 31st of January occurring after the tax year in which the loss arose.

****

Chapter 5

Business Equipment-Capital Allowances

Most businesses, in order to operate efficiently and effectively, will require some sort of equipment and, in many cases, vehicles of one sort or another. As we have seen, the cost of these items cannot be deducted as an expense when calculating profits. Instead, capital allowances must be claimed. If you are a small business that has opted to prepare cash accounts, then you do not have to calculate capital allowances when you buy equipment. In most cases, you can quite simply deduct the payment from your business receipts.

You can claim capital allowances when you buy assets that you keep to use in your business, e.g:

- equipment
- machinery
- business vehicles, e.g. cars, vans or lorries

These are commonly known as plant and machinery. You can deduct some or all the value of the item from your profits before you pay tax.

Other capital allowances

As well as plant and machinery, you can also claim capital allowances for:

- renovating business premises in disadvantaged areas of the UK.
- extracting minerals.
- research and development.
- 'know-how" (intellectual property about industrial techniques).
- patents.
- dredging.
- structures and buildings.

If you let out residential property
You can only claim for items in Residential property if your business qualifies as a furnished holiday lettings business. In each year the property must be:
- available for holiday letting for 210 days.
- let for 105 days or more.

What counts as plant and machinery
Plant and machinery includes:
- items that you keep to use in your business, including cars.
- costs of demolishing plant and machinery.
- parts of a building considered integral, known as 'integral features'.
- some fixtures, eg fitted kitchens or bathroom suites.
- alterations to a building to install other plant and machinery - this doesn't include repairs.

Integral features

Integral features are:
- lifts, escalators and moving walkways.
- space and water heating systems.
- air-conditioning and air cooling systems.
- hot and cold water systems (but not toilet and kitchen facilities).
- electrical systems, including lighting systems.
- external solar shading.

Fixtures

You can claim for fixtures, eg:
- fitted kitchens.
- bathroom suites.
- fire alarm and CCTV systems.

You can claim if you rent or own the building, but only the person who bought the item can claim. When you buy a building from a previous business owner you can only claim for integral features and fixtures that they claimed for. You must agree the value of the fixtures with the seller. If you don't you can't claim for them. Agreeing the value also means the person selling the assets can account correctly for them.

If you let residential property

You can only claim for items in residential property if either:
- you run a furnished holiday lettings business.

- the item is in the common parts of a residential building, eg a table in the hallway of a block of flats.
- there are special rules if you run a care business.

Annual investment allowance

You can deduct the full value of an item that qualifies for annual investment allowance (AIA) from your profits before tax. You can claim AIA on most plant and machinery up to the AIA amount. The AIA amount is currently £1,000.000 (2023) and increases each 12 month period.

What you can't claim on

You can't claim AIA on:
- cars.
- items you owned for another reason before you started using them in your business.
- items given to you or your business.
- Claim writing down allowances instead.

When you can claim

You can only claim AIA in the period you bought the item. The date you bought it is:
- when you signed the contract, if payment is due within less than 4 months.
- when payment's due, if it's due more than 4 months later.

If you buy something under a hire purchase contract, you can claim for the payments you haven't made yet when you start using the item. You can't claim on the interest payments. If your business closes, you can't claim AIA for items bought in the final accounting period.

If you don't want to claim the full cost
If you don't want to claim the full cost, eg you have low profits, you can claim:
- writing down allowances instead
- part of the cost as AIA and part as writing down allowances

Items you also use outside your business
You can't claim the full value of items you also use outside your business if you're a sole trader or partner. Reduce the capital allowances you claim by the amount you use the asset outside your business.

If you spend more than the AIA amount
Claim writing down allowances on any amount above the AIA. If a single item takes you above the AIA amount you can split the value between the types of allowance.

Mixed partnerships
AIA isn't available for partnerships where one of the partners is a company or another partnership.

More than one business or trade

If you're a sole trader or a partner and you have more than one business or trade, each business usually gets an AIA. You only get one AIA if the businesses are both:
- controlled by the same person.
- in the same premises or have similar activities.

If 2 or more limited companies are controlled by the same person, they only get one AIA between them. They can choose how to share the AIA.

First year allowances

If you buy an asset that qualifies for first year allowances, you can deduct the full cost from your profits before tax.

You can claim first year allowances in addition to annual investment allowance - they don't count towards your AIA limit. You can claim 'enhanced capital allowances' (a type of first year allowances) for the following energy and water efficient equipment:
- Electric cars and cars with zero CO_2 emissions.
- plant and machinery for gas re-fuelling stations, for example storage tanks, pumps.
- gas, biogas and hydrogen re-fueling equipment.
- zero-emission goods vehicles.
- equipment for electric vehicle charging points.
- plant and machinery for use in a freeport tax site, if you're a company.

You can't normally claim on items your business buys to lease to other people or for use within a home you let out. If you don't claim all the first year allowances you're entitled to, you can claim part of the cost in the next accounting period using writing down allowances.

Business cars

You can claim capital allowances on cars you buy and use in your business. This means you can deduct part of the value from your profits before you pay tax. Use writing down allowances to work out what you can claim - cars don't qualify for annual investment allowance (AIA).

Sole traders and partners

If you're a sole trader or a partner you can claim simplified mileage expenses on business vehicles instead - as long as you haven't already claimed for them in another way.

Employees

If you're an employee you can't claim capital allowances for cars, motorbikes and bicycles you use for work, but you may be able to claim for business mileage and fuel costs.

What counts as a car

For capital allowances a car is a type of vehicle that is suitable for private use - this includes motorhomes, vehicles most people use privately and those not built for transporting goods.

What doesn't count

Because they don't count as cars you can claim AIA on:
- motorcycles - apart from those bought before 6 April 2009.
- lorries, vans and trucks.

Rates for cars

The rate you can claim depends on the CO2 emissions of your car and the date you bought it. The main and special rates apply from 1 April for limited companies, and 6 April for sole traders and partners.

The first year allowances rate applies from 1 April for all businesses.

Cars bought from April 2021	
Description of car	What you can claim
New and unused, CO2 emissions are 0g/km (or car is electric)	First year allowances
New and unused, CO2 emissions are 50g/km or less or car is electric	Main rate allowances
Second hand, CO2 emissions are 50g/km or less (or car is electric)	Main rate allowances
New or second hand, CO2 emissions are above 50g/km	Special rate allowances
Cars bought between April 2018 and April 2021	

BUSINESS EQUIPMENT-CAPITAL ALLOWANCES

Description of car	What you can claim	
New and unused, CO_2 emissions are 50g/km or less (or car is electric)	First allowances	year
New and unused, CO_2 emissions are 110g/km or less or car is electric	Main allowances	rate
Second hand, CO_2 emissions are 110g/km or less (or car is electric)	Main allowances	rate
New or second hand, CO_2 emissions are above 110g/km	Special allowances	rate

Cars bought from April 2015-April 2018

Description of car	What you can claim	
New and unused, CO_2 emissions are 75g/km or less (or car is electric)	First allowances	year
New and unused, CO_2 emissions are 130g/km or less or car is electric	Main allowances	rate
Second hand, CO_2 emissions are 130g/km or less (or car is electric)	Main allowances	rate
New or second hand, CO_2 emissions are above 130g/km	Special allowances	rate

Cars bought between April 2013 and April 2015

Description of car	What you can claim	
New and unused, CO_2 emissions are 95g/km or less (or car is electric)	First allowances	year

New and unused, CO_2 emissions are between 95g/km and 130g/km	Main allowances	rate
Second hand, CO_2 emissions are 130g/km or less (or car is electric)	Main allowances	rate
New or second hand, CO_2 emissions are above 130g/km	Special allowances	rate

Cars bought between April 2009 and April 2013

Description of car	What you can claim	
New and unused, CO_2 emissions are 110g/km or less (or car is electric)	First year allowances	
New and unused, CO_2 emissions are between 110g/km and 160g/km	Main allowances	rate
Second hand, CO_2 emissions are 160g/km or less (or car is electric)	Main allowances	rate
New or second hand, CO_2 emissions above 160g/km	Special allowances	rate

Using cars outside your business

If you're a sole trader or partner and you also use your car outside your business, calculate how much you can claim based on the amount of business use. If your business provides a car for an employee or director, you can claim capital allowances on the full cost. You may need to report it as a benefit if they use it personally.

How to claim

When you've worked out your capital allowances, claim on your:
- Self Assessment tax return if you are a motor trader.
- partnership tax return if you're a partner.
- Company Tax Return if you're a limited company - you must include a separate capital allowances calculation.

The amount you can claim is deducted from your profits.

When you can claim

You must claim in the accounting period you bought the item if you want to claim the full value under:
- annual investment allowance.
- first year allowances.

If you don't want to claim the full value you can claim part of it using writing down allowances. You can do this at any time as long as you still own the item.

When you bought it

The date you bought it is:
- when you signed the contract, if payment is due within less than 4 months.
- when payment's due, if it's due more than 4 months later.

If you buy something under a hire purchase contract you can claim for the payments you haven't made yet when you start using the item. You can't claim on the interest payments.

Chapter 6

Giving to Charity

Overview

Your limited company pays less Corporation Tax when it gives the following to charity:
- money
- equipment or trading stock (items it makes or sells)
- land, property or shares in another company (shares in your own company don't qualify)
- employees (on secondment)
- sponsorship payments

You can claim tax relief by deducting the value of your donations from your total business profits before you pay tax.

Different rules for sole traders and partnerships.
Donations by individuals to charity or to community amateur sports clubs (CASCs) are tax free. This is called tax relief. The tax goes to you or the charity. How this works depends on whether you donate:
- through Gift Aid
- straight from your wages or pension through a Payroll Giving scheme

- land, property or shares
- in your will

This also applies to sole traders and partnerships. There are different rules for limited companies.

If you want to donate to a sports club, check if it's registered as a community amateur sports club (CASC). You cannot donate to a CASC through Payroll Giving.

Donating money

Your limited company can pay less Corporation Tax when it gives money to a charity or community amateur sports club (CASC). Deduct the value of the donations from your total business profits before you pay tax.

Payments that don't qualify

You can't deduct payments that:
- are loans that will be repaid by the charity
- are made on the condition that the charity will buy property from your company or anyone connected with it
- are a distribution of company profits (eg dividends)

If you're given something in return

Any benefits you're given in return for your donation (eg tickets to an event) must be below a certain value.

Donation amount	Maximum value of benefit
Up to £100	25% of the donation
£101 - £1,000	£25
£1,001 and over	5% of the donation (up to a maximum of £2,500)

This applies to benefits given to any person or company connected with your company, including close relatives. If you get a benefit that's related to the company your donation qualifies as a sponsorship payment.

Equipment and trading stock

Your limited company pays less Corporation Tax if it gives equipment or items it makes or sells ('trading stock') to a charity or community amateur sports club (CASC).

Giving equipment

You can claim full capital allowances on the cost of equipment. To qualify, the equipment must have been used by your company. This includes things like:
- office furniture
- computers and printers
- vans and cars
- tools and machinery

Giving trading stock

If your company donates its trading stock to a charity or CASC, you don't have to include anything in your sales income for the value of the gift. This means you get tax relief on the cost of the stock you've given away.

VAT

If your company is VAT-registered, you'll need to account for VAT on the items you give away. However, you can apply zero VAT to the items - even if you normally charge the standard or reduced rate - if your company makes the donation specifically so that the charity can:
- sell the items
- hire out the items
- export the items

This means you can reclaim the VAT on the cost of the trading stock you donate. If you can't zero rate the items, use the VAT rate you normally apply to them.

Land, property and shares

Your limited company could pay less Corporation Tax if it gives or sells any of the following to charity:
- land or property
- shares in another company

You can't claim for gifts or sales of shares in your own company.

Contact your chosen charity first to make sure it can accept your gift.

What you get
If you give these to charity (including selling them for less than they're worth):
- you won't have to pay tax on capital gains
- you can deduct the value of the gift (its 'market value') from your business profits before you pay tax

If you donate or sell to a community amateur sports club (CASC), you don't pay tax on capital gains but you can't deduct the value of the gift from your business profits.

Work out the market value
You'll need to know how much the gift would sell for in an open market (its 'market value') to calculate your tax relief. You can get professional help with this.

What you need to do
You must keep documents relating to the donation to show that you've made the gift or sale and that the charity has accepted it. You must keep these records for at least 6 years.

Land or property
You must get a letter or certificate from the charity which contains:
- a description of the land or property
- the date of the gift or sale (the 'disposal date')

- a statement confirming that it now owns the land or property

Shares

You must fill in a stock transfer form to take the shares out of your company's name and put them into the charity's name.

Selling land, property or shares on behalf of a charity

When you offer a gift of land, property or shares, the charity may ask you to sell the gift on its behalf. You can do this and still claim tax relief for the donation, but you must keep records of the gift and the charity's request. Without them, you might have to pay Corporation Tax.

Seconding employees

You can deduct any costs as normal business expenses if:
- your company temporarily transfers an employee to work for a charity (known as a 'secondment')
- an employee volunteers for a charity in work time

Your company must continue to pay the employee and run Pay As You Earn (PAYE) on their salary. You can set the costs (including wages and business expenses) against your taxable profits as if they were still working for you.

You can't claim the costs of employees on secondment or volunteering at a community amateur sports club (CASC).

Sponsoring a charity

Charity sponsorship payments are different from donations because your company gets something related to the business in return. You can deduct sponsorship payments from your business profits before you pay tax by treating them as business expenses.

What qualifies

Payments qualify as business expenses if the charity:
- publicly supports your products or services
- allows you to use their logo in your own printed material
- allows you to sell your goods or services at their event or premises
- links from their website to yours

If you're unsure whether a charity payment qualifies as a sponsorship payment or a donation, contact the charities helpline.

Telephone:
0300 123 1073

How to claim

There are different ways to claim tax relief depending on the type of donation you make.

Deduct from your profits
Claim relief in the Company Tax Return that covers the accounting period during which you made the donation or sale if you have:
- donated money
- given or sold land, property or shares

Enter the total value of your donations in the 'Qualifying donations' box of the 'Deductions and Reliefs' section of your tax return. There are special rules for working out the value of your donation if you give or sell land, property or shares to a charity.

Deduct as business expenses
Deduct costs as normal business expenses in your company's annual accounts if you have:
- seconded employees
- sponsored a charity

Claim capital allowances
Claim capital allowances on the cost of equipment you donate in your company's annual accounts.

If you donate more than your profit
The most you can deduct is the amount that reduces your company's profits to zero. If you donate more than your total profits you can't:

- declare trading losses on your tax return
- carry over any remaining amount to your next tax return

****

Chapter 7

Paying for Employees

As we have discussed, taking on employees constitutes a major expense and also an administrative burden. Obviously, when you take on employee(s) it is for the reason that you see that your business, whether a company, sole trader, or partnership can prosper by their employment.

There is an awful lot of information to absorb when becoming an employer, and it is for this reason that most employees instruct their accountant (at an extra cost) to operate a PAYE system for them and to administer any statutory payments, as outlined below.

Taxes to pay when employing someone

As an employer you are responsible for the following:

- Paying all employees at least the Minimum Wage/National Living Wage as below:

Year	21 and over	18-20	Under 18 And Apprentices
April 2024/25 (current rate)	£11.44	£8.60	£6.40

- Deducting Income tax and Class 1 National Insurance from their wages through the PAYE system
- Paying employer's Class 1 national Insurance Contributions
- Operating any other payments, statutory payments as due, such as Statutory Sick pay (SSP)
- Statutory maternity pay (SMP) see below, Statutory Paternity Pay (OSPP) and Statutory Adoption Pay (SAP).
- The administration and deduction of any student loan payments
- Notifying HMRC about any perks and benefits so that employee's can be taxed on them and paying the relevant NI contributions on those perks.

Statutory Maternity Pay and leave

Eligible employees can take up to 52 weeks' maternity leave. The first 26 weeks is known as 'Ordinary Maternity Leave', the last 26 weeks as 'Additional Maternity Leave'. The earliest that leave can be taken is 11 weeks before the expected week of childbirth, unless the baby is born early. Employees must take at least 2 weeks after the birth (or 4 weeks if they're a factory worker).

Statutory Maternity Pay (SMP)

SMP for eligible employees can be paid for up to 39 weeks, usually as follows:

- the first 6 weeks: 90% of their average weekly earnings (AWE) before tax
- the remaining 33 weeks: £172.48 (2023/2024) or 90% of their AWE (whichever is lower)

Tax and National Insurance needs to be deducted.

Statutory Paternity Pay and leave

Employees may be eligible for Statutory Paternity Leave and Pay if they and their partner are:
- having a baby
- adopting a child
- having a baby through a surrogacy arrangement

Statutory Paternity Leave

Employees can choose to take either 1 week or 2 consecutive weeks' leave. The amount of time is the same even if they have more than one child (eg twins). Leave can't start before the birth. The start date must be one of the following:

- the actual date of birth
- an agreed number of days after the birth
- an agreed number of days after the expected week of childbirth

Leave must finish within 56 days of the birth (or due date if the baby is early). The start and end dates are different if the employee is adopting.

Statutory Paternity Pay

Statutory Paternity Pay for eligible employees is either £172.48 a week (2023/2024) or 90% of their average weekly earnings (whichever is lower). Tax and National Insurance need to be deducted. Most people who work for you will be classed as an employee. Those who provide you with services are self-employed and look after their own tax and NI. HMRC will take a view as to whether a person that you engage is self-employed or employed. If in any doubt it is always best to clarify with HMRC via their helpline 0300 200 3300.

Shared parental leave

Employees and their partners may be able to get Shared Parental Leave (SPL) and Statutory Shared Parental Pay (ShPP) if they are having a baby or adopting a child. They can share up to 50 weeks of leave and up to 37 weeks of pay between them. They need to share the pay and leave in the first year after their child is born or placed with their family. They can use SPL to take leave in blocks separated by periods of work, or take it all in one go. They can also choose to be off work together or to stagger the leave and pay.

Adoption pay

Statutory Adoption Pay is paid for up to 39 weeks. The weekly amount is:
- 90% of average weekly earnings for the first 6 weeks
- £172.48 or 90% of average weekly earnings (whichever is lower) for the next 33 weeks

It's paid in the same way as wages (eg monthly or weekly). Tax and National Insurance will be deducted.

Company directors

Company directors are almost always classed as employees and their salaries are taxed as normal under the PAYE system. However, there are special rules relating to the National insurance paid by directors.

You can find out more information by visiting www.gov.uk/employee-directors which outlines the NI responsibilities.

Sometimes, family members work for a business and it will be necessary to decide on their status. Family members living in the same household do not need to be paid the NMW/Living Wage.

Self-employed or a partner

If you work in the capacity of self-employed or are a partner in a business, then any amounts you choose to take from yourself or partnership are known as drawings and they are not a a wage or salary. This is different to a director when money taken is salary and must be taxed under PAYE or paid as dividends which in turn are taxable.

Registering as an employer

As we have seen, if you have employees, you must operate a PAYE scheme for deduction of all taxes, loans, statutory payments etc. When taking on employees and starting a PAYE scheme you should regsiter with HMRC at https://www.gov.uk/new-business-register-for-tax.

For further assistance you can call the employers helpline on 0300 200 3200. There is also a Support for new employers helpline 0300 200 3211

Once you have registered with HMRC you will need to maintain the correct records and, as most filing is now done online, you will need the appropriate software. HMRC provide free software to help you with basic calculations, such as pay and deductions. However, if you have a number of employees then you will need to purchase software. Information on suitable software can be obtained from HMRC https://www.gov.uk/payroll-software.

Operating a payroll scheme

Once you have registered with HMRC you will need to master the basics of operating the PAYE scheme, unless your accountant is doing it for you. It is still advisable to know even if this is the case. One of the best sites to visit is www.gov.uk/paye-for-employers. This provides advice and guidance.

The basic steps are as follows:
- Every time you pay an employee the payment will fall into a designated month or week, depending on whether they are paid monthly or weekly.

- Every employee has a tax code allocated by HMRC. Tax codes denote the amount of tax deducted (or refunded) for the period in question.
- A deduction is made for employers and employee's National Insurance.
- In certain cases, statutory payments are calculated and added to the employee's pay.
- A P11 form is filled in recording all payments to the individual. The P11 will show the cumulative pay to date and also the National Insurance Number and tax coding.
- Each time an employee is paid, they have to be supplied with a pay slip summarising the details on the P11, their net pay and any other adjustments such as pensions. Under Real Time Processing a Full Payment Submission must be supplied. Real Time processing simply means data that is submitted at the time of collection but information is sent to HMRC before deductions are actually made. For more information on Real Time data, you should contact the HMRC employers helpline. Again, this is an area where you would probably need expert assistance, such as your accountant operating payroll for you.

At the end of each month, you will need to pay HMRC the amounts due to them. For those whose payments are less than £1500 there is an option of a quarterly payment. At the end of each tax year, you will need to supply your employees with a P60 for summarizing all pay and taxes for the year. Also, staff in receipt of any perks must receive a form P11D, sometimes a P9D.

Taking on a new member of staff

You must tell HM Revenue and Customs (HMRC) when you take on a new employee and be registered as an employer. Before you pay your new starter follow these steps.
- Get employee information to work out their tax code - if you don't have their P45, use HMRC's 'starter checklist' (which replaced the P46).
- Find out if they need to repay a student loan.
- Use these details to set up your new employee in your payroll software.
- Register your employee with HMRC using a Full Payment Submission (FPS).

You must also follow the same steps as when you start employing staff for the first time, eg checking they can work in the UK.

Check you need to pay someone through PAYE

You usually have to pay your employees through PAYE if they earn £123 or more a week (£533 a month or £6396 a year). (2023/24) You don't need to pay self-employed workers through PAYE.

Working out if someone is an employee or self-employed

As a general rule, someone is:

- employed if they work for you and don't have any of the risks associated with running a business.
- self-employed if they run their own business and are responsible for its success or failure.

You must check each worker's employment status to make sure they're not self-employed. If you get it wrong you may have to pay extra tax, National Insurance, interest and a penalty.

Temporary or agency workers

You need to operate PAYE on temporary workers that you pay directly, as long as they're classed as an employee. You don't need to operate PAYE if a worker is paid by an agency, unless the agency's based abroad and doesn't have a trading address or representative in the UK. There are special rules for harvest workers or shoot beaters employed for less than 2 weeks.

Employees you only pay once

You operate PAYE differently for employees you only pay once. Set up a payroll record with their full name and address. If you give them a payroll ID, make sure it's unique. Give your employee a statement showing their pay before and after deductions, and the payment date, eg a payslip or a letter. Don't give them a P45.

Volunteers

You don't need to operate PAYE on volunteers if they only get expenses that aren't subject to tax or National Insurance - check if their expenses are affected.

Students

Operate PAYE on students in the same way as you do for other employees.

Get employee information

You need to get certain information from your employee so you can set them up with the correct tax code and starter declaration on your payroll software.

You'll usually get most of this information from the employee's P45, but they'll have to fill in a 'starter checklist' (which replaced the P46 form) if they don't have a recent P45.

You'll need your employee's:
- date of birth
- gender
- full address
- start date.

From your employee's P45, you'll need their:

- full name
- leaving date from their last job
- total pay and tax paid to date for the current tax year
- student loan deduction status
- National Insurance number
- existing tax code

You must keep this information in your payroll records for the current year and the 3 following tax years. If your employee doesn't have a P45, ask your employee for this information if you don't have their P45, or if they left their last job before 6 April 2015. The P46 form is no longer used. Get the information by asking your new employee to complete HMRC's new starter checklist. They'll need to save it on their computer and open and complete it in Adobe Reader version 9.0 or later.

If your employee has more than one P45

You should use the P45 with the latest date and give the other one back to the employee. If they have the same leaving date use the P45 with the highest tax free allowance (or least additional pay for a K code) and give the other one back to the employee.

Work out your employee's tax code

Use the information to work out their tax code and starter declaration. You need these to set them up on your payroll software and register them with HMRC. There's a different way to work out tax codes for employees seconded from abroad or who you only pay once.

Understanding tax codes

For more information on what exactly a tax code means and how it applies to your employees (or indeed yourself) you should go to:
https://www.gov.uk/employee-tax-codes/letters.

Student loan repayments

You should make student loan deductions if any of the following apply:
- your new employee's P45 shows that deductions should continue.
- your new employee tells you they're repaying a student loan, eg on a starter checklist.

HM Revenue and Customs (HMRC) sends you form SL1 and your employee earns over the income threshold for their repayment plan

What you need to do

If your new employee needs you to make student loan repayments, record this in your payroll software. It will automatically calculate and make deductions. Report these deductions to HMRC when you pay your employee.

Special rules

In some cases, there are special rules for making student loan deductions.

Examples include:
- you're sent a court order to collect a debt directly from your employee's earnings.
- you change how often you pay your employee, such as from weekly to monthly.
- the employee has more than one job with you and you need to aggregate earnings

Stopping deductions

HMRC will send you form SL2 if you need to stop deducting student loan repayments from your employee's pay. Don't stop making deductions if an employee asks you to.

Registering your new employee

Register your new employee with HM Revenue and Customs (HMRC) by including their details on a Full Payment Submission (FPS) the first time you pay them. On this FPS, include:
- information you've collected from them
- the tax code and starter declaration that you've worked out
- pay and deductions (eg tax, National Insurance and student loan deductions) since they started working for you - don't include figures from their previous job

Taxing Perks-Benefits in kind

Employers will sometimes provide memebers of staff with perks or benefits in kind. Perks are usually applicable to larger businesses such as company cars or medical insurance, cars and childcare. However, smaller employers can also provide certain perks that may be taxable.

If you receive any other benefits as part of your employment in addition to your salary, it may be the case that you are receiving a benefit-in-kind (BIK). You might see it as a workplace perk, or sometimes they're referred to as 'fringe benefits', but what you need to be aware of is that although they can seem like a nice added bonus, they may not necessarily come for free.

What is a benefit-in-kind?

Common examples of BIKs can include access to a company car, which you're also allowed for personal use – such as driving your kids to school and going shopping, private medical insurance or even free canteen meals. In essence, anything that has been provided to you which is not "wholly, exclusively, and necessary" for you to perform your employment duties is considered a BIK. However, BIKs can be split into two groups – those THAT attract tax and those which are tax-free. We explain these below.

What are tax-free benefits-in-kind? Tax-free BIKs are possibly the most common benefits you're likely to encounter, for the very reason that they are tax-free. Neither the employee nor the employer is required to pay additional tax as a result of these benefits.

The below is not an exhaustive list but just some of the most popular that you're likely to come across:

- Employer contributions to an approved workplace or personal pension scheme.
- Subsidised canteen meals so long as this is offered to all employees.
- In-house leisure facilities such as gym, pool table or other entertainment.
- Other in-house facilities such as childcare services at your place of work.
- Staff parties so long as every employee is invited and cost per person is not over £150 per year.
- Bicycles and cycling equipment as part of the Cycle to Work scheme.
- Gifts for reasons that are unconnected to the performance of your job such as birthday, wedding or retirement (but the value of these gifts should not exceed £250 in a single year).
- Trivial benefits which are less than £50 in value and are not cash or cash voucher such as free coffee and tea in the office.
- Office or workplace car park.
- Uniform or safety equipment provided which is necessary for you to complete your job.

What are taxable benefits-in-kind?

- Other benefits which do not make up part of your taxable earnings may still, however, be of generous value. Therefore, in order to prevent employers from reducing employees' salaries and topping it up with free benefits, the government imposes employer's national insurance (NI) and employee's income tax to be paid on some BIKs. Again, the below is not a complete list but some of the most common BIKs and an explanation of when they will attract tax:
- Company car where you are allowed to use it for personal use. The total value of this benefit will take into consideration the list price of the car, the vehicle's carbon dioxide emissions, the type of fuel the car uses (except for pure electric vehicles) and the date of registration of the car.
- Fuel for the company car is provided by your employer and you are free to use it for your personal use.
- Accommodation which has been provided rent-free or below market rent **AND** where you are not required to live there in order to perform your job role.
- Non-specific regular clothing or clothing allowance which means clothing that is not specifically required in order for you to carry out your job such as protective goggles. Often this can also be determined as clothing that you would also wear outside of work.
- Private medical insurance.

- School fees for employees' children.
- Interest-free or cheap loans provided to you as an employee from the company or business where the amount is over £10,000.
- Holidays or holiday vouchers

There are different and complex rules on what kind of tax needs to be paid, and by who, depending on what benefit is being offered/received and how it has been administered. In general, BIKs can attract income tax, employer's NI and employee's NI.

An employee who receives a BIK will be charged income tax. To calculate how much, the employee needs to apply their personal income tax rate band (20% for basic rate, 40% for higher rate or 45% for additional rate) to the taxable value of the benefit, which HMRC defines as the cash equivalent. This means that, if it costs the employer £600 per year to provide an employee with gym membership and they are a basic rate taxpayer, they will need to pay 20% of £600 as income tax on this benefit.

Employers who provide BIKs to their employees will also need to pay tax in the form of employer's NI at a rate of 13.8%. Again, this is applied to the taxable value of the benefit. However, the cost to provide BIKs is an allowable tax-deductible expense which means it can be taken off profits for corporation tax purposes. Employers may choose to offer

BIKs as a more affordable way to reward staff than through their salary.

In most instances, although an employee may have to pay income tax on the BIK, they will not have to pay NI on it which is one tax saving they make. To ensure BIKs do not attract employee NI, it is important to administer the benefit in a way where the employee is not receiving cash or equivalent such as vouchers – as this will be treated as earnings and be liable to both income tax and employee NI.

How do I report and pay for tax on a benefit-in-kind?
The responsibility to declare the BIKs that have been received by employees is on the employer. To do this they must complete and submit the P11D form to HMRC by 6 July following the tax year in which the benefits were received. For example, if an employee was in receipt of BIKs between 6 April 2022 to 5 April 2023, the P11D form deadline would be 6 July 2024. The form provides a list of all possible benefits which the employer simply selects the relevant ones and states the value of the benefit that was provided to the employee. A copy of this form should also be provided to the employee.

Employers will also need to complete the P11D(b) form which can be accessed through the HMRC Government Gateway. The P11D(b) form must be submitted alongside the P11D and this allows for employers to pay their NI on the BIKs.

For employees, income tax is charged on the BIK. The payment for this will be automatically deducted via their payroll and so there is nothing they need to do. However, when an employer provides them with a copy of the P11D, they should double check that the benefits and value have been reported as expected. If there are any discrepancies, they will need to raise this with their payroll as soon as possible.

****

Chapter 8

Business Premises

It is important to know the ins and outs of operating your business from premises, or from home. It is obviously cheaper to operate from home but you need to know the tax situation and also the situation concerning business rates. In addition, you need to know about buying business premises and also eventually selling the premises.

Operating a business from home

There are an increasing number of people operating businesses from home. You can claim for space used, using a simple calculation based on the overall numbers of rooms in your house or square meters. You then need to calculate what space you use for working and then apportion the overall running costs of your home to arrive at a figure.

Running costs will typically be lighting, heating and landline plus council tax. Internet connections should be allocated to your business as opposed to personal use. Home insurance policies can be apportioned and business insurance claimed in its entirety. In addition, a proportion of your mortgage interest can be claimed. However, you will need further advice in this area. See the simple example below concerning electricity costs which will give you an idea of apportionment.

Example You have 4 rooms in your home, one of which you use only as an office.

Your electricity bill for the year is £400. Assuming all the rooms in your home use equal amounts of electricity, you can claim £100 as allowable expenses (£400 divided by 4).

If you worked only one day a week from home, you could claim £14.29 as allowable expenses (£100 divided by 7).

However, if you want to avoid using complex formulas to calculate what you can claim you can use a system of 'Simplified expenses' introduced by HMRC which allows you to use a flat rate. For details of simplified expenses and the flat rates you should go to https://www.gov.uk/simpler-income-tax-simplified-expenses.

This will provide all details of this system of claiming expenditure.

Renting a business premises

You will be entitled to claim for all costs incurred in relation to a business premises such as:
- Rent for the premises.
- Business rates.
- Water rates.
- Utilities (heat and power).
- Insurances.

- Repair costs.
- Legal and other professional fees.

If you have any other costs, such as security, then these can also be deducted. If you have premises which also include a flat, then business rates will be applicable on the business element and council tax on the residential element. Any other expenses will also need to be apportioned and be included on your tax return.

Purchasing a business property

For many people, the most favourable situation is to purchase a business premises. However, when you purchase there will be a stamp duty land tax to pay. You pay SDLT on increasing portions of the property price (or 'consideration') when you pay £150,000 or more for non-residential or mixed-use land or property. You must still send an SDLT return for most transactions under £150,000. Non-residential property includes:

- commercial property, eg shops or offices.
- agricultural land.
- Forests.
- any other land or property which is not used as a residence.
- 6 or more residential properties bought in a single transaction.

A 'mixed use' property is one that has both residential and non-residential elements, eg a flat connected to a shop, doctor's surgery or office.

Freehold sales and transfers

You can use the table below to work out the SDLT rate or a lease premium.

Property or lease premium or transfer value	SDLT rate
Up to £150,000	Zero
The next £100,000 (the portion from £150,001 to £250,000)	2%
The remaining amount (the portion above £250,000)	5%

Example-If you buy a freehold commercial property for £275,000, the SDLT you owe is calculated as follows:
- 0% on the first £150,000 = £0
- 2% on the next £100,000 = £2,000
- 5% on the final £25,000 = £1,250
- Total SDLT = £3,250

New leasehold sales and transfers

When you buy a new non-residential or mixed use leasehold you pay SDLT on both the:
- purchase price of the lease (the 'lease premium') using the rates above
- value of the annual rent you pay (the 'net present value')

These are calculated separately then added together.

If you buy an existing ('assigned') lease, you only pay SDLT on the lease price (or 'consideration'). The net present value (NPV) is based on the total rent over the life of the lease. You don't pay SDLT on the rent if the NPV is less than £150,000.

Net present value of rent	SDLT rate
£0 to £150,000	Zero
The portion from £150,001 to £5,000,000	1%
The portion above £5,000,000	2%

How much you'll pay

You may pay a higher rate of SDLT for multiple purchases or transfers from the same seller.

Financing your property

Most people buying commercial premises will require a loan or mortgage to purchase the property. There are two aspects to a business mortgage and both are treated differently for tax purposes as follows:
- You can claim relief on the interest charged on the loan.
- You cannot claim the ongoing mortgage payments, i.e. the capital sum.

However, there may be other ways of claiming payments as an expense, such as funding the repayments with a pension mortgage as the premiums attract relief. You would need to consult your accountant or a financial adviser to get more information. If you buy a property outright you cannot claim tax relief although there are capital allowances and fixtures to take into account (see below).

Selling a business property

You may get tax relief if you sell property that you use for business. This may reduce or delay the amount of Capital Gains Tax you pay. If the purpose of your business is to buy and sell property (you're a property developer, for example) you don't pay Capital Gains Tax when you sell a property. Instead, you pay:

- Income Tax - if you're a sole trader or partner.
- Corporation Tax - if you're a limited company.

There are special rules for limited companies that dispose of a single residential property worth more than £2 million.

More information can be found at https://www.gov.uk/tax-sell-property/businesses.

Capital allowances

As mentioned, income tax and corporation tax relief may be available on the purchase of a property.

Leases of property

In many cases, the premises that you purchase will be leasehold. If you pay an up-front premium, a lease premium, to the landlord or outgoing tenant, if the lease is less than 50 years you may be able to claim a deduction against your trading profits for part of the premium for each year.

VAT

Value Added tax on the purchase of land and buildings is complicated and you will need to obtain advice from HMRC in this area. Briefly, new freehold commercial and industrial buildings which are less than three years old are liable to VAT at the standard rate. Land and the sale and lease of commercial buildings are exempt unless the person selling has exercised an option to charge it.

Disposing of business property

When you sell property used in a business you will incur a capital gains liability if the amount that you sell for is more than the amount you paid for it. If the amount that you sell for is less than the amount paid you will have made a capital loss and you can claim this, or set it off, against any future capital gains you make.

Two important points to remember here:
- If you trade as a limited company, the gain will be reduced by what is known as an indexation allowance.

Capital gains tax is paid as part of corporation tax liability.

- If you are a sole trader or partner, you will only be able to claim entrepreneur's relief if the sale is part of all or part of your business as a going concern. Sales of assets in isolation do not qualify for this relief.

Business Asset Disposal Relief

You may also qualify for Business Asset Disposal Relief (BADR), (formerly known as Entrepreneurs relief before April 2020). BADR means you'll pay tax at 10% on all gains on qualifying assets.

If you're selling all or part of your business

To qualify for relief, both of the following must apply for at least 2 years up to the date you sell your business:

- you're a sole trader or business partner.
- you've owned the business for at least 2 years.

The same conditions apply if you're closing your business instead. You must also dispose of your business assets within 3 years to qualify for relief.

If you're selling shares or securities

- To qualify, both of the following must apply for at least 2 years up to the date you sell your shares:
- you're an employee or office holder of the company (or one in the same group).

- the company's main activities are in trading (rather than non-trading activities like investment) - or it's the holding company of a trading group.
- There are also other rules depending on whether or not the shares are from an Enterprise Management Incentive (EMI).

If the shares are from an EMI
- You must have both:
- bought the shares after 5 April 2013.
- been given the option to buy them at least 2 years before selling them.

If the shares are not from an EMI
- For at least 2 years before you sell your shares, the business must be a 'personal company'. This means that you have at least 5% of both the:
- Shares.
- voting rights.
- You must also be entitled to at least 5% of either:
- profits that are available for distribution and assets on winding up the company.
- disposal proceeds if the company is sold.
- If the number of shares you hold falls below 5% because the company has issued more shares, you may still be able to claim Business Asset Disposal Relief.

- You need to choose or 'elect' to be treated as if you had sold and re-bought your shares immediately before the new shares were issued. This will create a gain on which you can claim Business Asset Disposal Relief.
- You can also choose or 'elect' to postpone paying tax on that gain until you come to sell your shares.
- You can do this by:
- completing the additional information section of the Capital Gains summary form of your tax return.
- writing to HMRC if you do not. have to complete a tax return for the year

If the company stops being a trading company

- If the company stops being a trading company, you can still qualify for relief if you sell your shares within 3 years.

If you're selling assets you lent to the business

- To qualify, both of the following must apply:
- you've sold at least 5% of your part of a business partnership or your shares in a personal company.
- you owned the assets but let your business partnership or personal company use them for at least one year up to the date you sold your business or shares - or the date the business closed.

If you're a trustee
- You may also qualify if you're a trustee selling assets held in the trust.
- For more details on the rules surrounding BADR go to
- https://www.gov.uk/business-asset-disposal-relief.

Rollover relief
You may be able to delay paying Capital Gains Tax if you:
- sell (or 'dispose of') some business assets.
- use all or part of the proceeds to buy new assets.
- Business Asset Rollover Relief means you won't pay any tax until you sell the new asset. You may then need to pay tax on the gain from the original asset. You can also claim:
- provisional relief if you're planning to buy new assets with your proceeds but haven't done it yet.
- relief if you use the proceeds to improve assets you already own.

Eligibility
To qualify for Business Asset Rollover Relief:
- you must buy the new assets within 3 years of selling or disposing of the old ones (or up to one year before)
- your business must be trading when you sell the old assets and buy the new ones.
- you must use the old and new assets in your business.
- You can claim relief on assets including:

- land and buildings.
- fixed plant or machinery, eg a printing press.

Partial relief

There are different rules if:
- you only reinvest part of the proceeds from selling the old assets.
- the old assets were only partly used in your business.
- you use the proceeds to buy 'depreciating assets' (fixed plant or machinery, or assets expected to last for less than 60 years)

Get help from a professional, eg an accountant or tax adviser, if you need advice.

How to claim

Fill in the form at the end of HM Revenue and Customs' (HMRC) helpsheet HS290 Business asset roll-over relief and include it with your Self Assessment tax return.

You must claim relief within 4 years of the end of the tax year when you bought the new asset (or sold the old one, if that happened after).

Example If you sell or dispose of the old asset in May 2018 and buy the new asset in August 2020, you need to claim relief by 5 April 2025.

SEED Enterprise Investment Scheme Relief

The Seed Enterprise Investment Scheme (SEIS) is designed to help small, early-stage companies raise equity finance by offering tax reliefs to individual investors who purchase new shares in those companies. It complements the existing BADR scheme which offers tax relief to investors in higher-risk small companies. SEIS is intended to recognise the particular difficulties which very early stage companies face in attracting investment, by offering tax relief at a higher rate. https://www.gov.uk/guidance/venture-capital-schemes-raise-money-by-offering-tax-reliefs-to-investors

****

Chapter 9

Dealing with VAT

Charging VAT

You can only charge VAT if your business is registered for VAT. VAT is charged on things like:

- business sales - for example when you sell goods and services.
- hiring or loaning goods to someone.
- selling business assets.
- Commission.
- items sold to staff - for example canteen meals.
- business goods used for personal reasons.
- 'non-sales' like bartering, part-exchange and gifts.

These are known as 'taxable supplies'. There are different rules for charities.

Responsibilities

VAT-registered businesses:
- must charge VAT on their goods or services.
- may reclaim any VAT they've paid on business-related goods or services

If you're a VAT-registered business, you must report to HM Revenue and Customs (HMRC) the amount of VAT you've charged and the amount of VAT you've paid. This is done through your VAT Return which is usually due every 3 months. You must account for VAT on the full value of what you sell, even if you:

- receive goods or services instead of money (eg if you take something in part-exchange).
- haven't charged any VAT to the customer - whatever price you charge is treated as including VAT.

If you've charged more VAT than you've paid, you have to pay the difference to HMRC. If you've paid more VAT than you've charged, you can reclaim the difference from HMRC.

Making Tax Digital

HMTC's Making Tax Digital (MTD) is the biggest shake up of tax laws in a generation, bringing tax into the digital age. From April 2024 all VAT registered businesses (with turnover over £90,000) will need to keep electronic records of their transactions. They will also have to submit their VAT data to HMRC digitally. This has to be done with MTD compliant software, or 'Functionally Compatible Software'. You can sign up voluntarily now before 2024 by going to:

https://www.gov.uk/guidance/sign-up-your-business-for-making-tax-digital-for-income-tax

What is 'functional compatible software'?

'Functional compatible software' is the cornerstone of MTD for VAT.

It will be used to maintain the compulsory digital records, calculate the return and submit it to HMRC via an application programme interface (API). Functional compatible software is simply the name given to a software program or set of compatible software programs which are capable of:

- recording and preserving records in an electronic form providing information and returns from the records to HMRC in an electronic form using the API platform.
- receiving information from HMRC.

It's possible to mix and match software – the complete set of digital records needed for MTD for VAT don't need to be held in one piece of software. As long as there is a link between the different pieces of software, the records can be held in a range of acceptable digital formats.

The link between the software is key and is a legal requirement where a set of compatible software programs is used. HMRC is likely to produce a list of software from commercial software suppliers which can be used for MTD for VAT.

Businesses whose turnover is less than £90,,000 are not required to be part of MTD at this stage but can join on a voluntary basis by getting in touch with HMRC.

VAT registered businesses not within the scope of MTD can carry on submitting VAT returns as before, using the online VAT return form on gov.uk.

For a list of exempt businesses (which are few such as Religious Societies) contact the VAT helpline on 0300 200 3700.

VAT rates

There are 3 different rates of VAT and you must make sure you charge the right amount.

Rate	% of VAT
Standard	20%
Reduced rate	5%
Zero rate	0%

Standard rate

Most goods and services are standard rate. You should charge this rate unless the goods or services are classed as reduced or zero-rated.

Reduced rate

When you charge this rate can depend on what the item is as well as the circumstances of the sale, for example:
- children's car seats and domestic fuel or power are always charged at 5%.

- mobility aids for older people are only charged at 5% if they're for someone over 60 and the goods are installed in their home.

Zero rate

Zero-rated means that the goods are still VAT-taxable but the rate of VAT you must charge your customers is 0%. You still have to record them in your VAT accounts and report them on your VAT Return. Examples include:
- books and newspapers.
- children's clothes and shoes.
- motorcycle helmets.
- most goods you export to non-EU countries.
- goods you supply to a VAT registered EU business - you can check if the VAT number is valid.

If you sent goods to the EU, you'll need their VAT number and paperwork proving that the goods have been sent within certain time limits (usually 3 months). Rates can change and you must apply any changes to the rates from the date they change.

What you must do when charging VAT

You need to know the right VAT rate so you can charge it correctly and reclaim it on your purchases. If a transaction is a standard, reduced or zero-rated taxable supply, you must:
- charge the right rate of VAT.
- work out the VAT if a single price is shown that includes or excludes VAT.

- show the VAT information on your invoice.
- show the transaction in your VAT account - a summary of your VAT.
- show the amount on your VAT Return

You may be able to reclaim the VAT on purchases that relate to these sales. You can't claim back all the amount you've paid if you pay the wrong amount of VAT on a purchase.

VAT-inclusive and exclusive prices

You'll need to make a calculation when charging VAT on goods or services, or when working out the amount of VAT you can claim back on items which were sold inclusive of VAT.

VAT-inclusive prices

To work out a price including the standard rate of VAT (20%), multiply the price excluding VAT by 1.2. To work out a price including the reduced rate of VAT (5%), multiply the price excluding VAT by 1.05.

When not to charge VAT

You can't charge VAT on exempt or 'out of scope' items. Some goods and services are outside the VAT tax system so you can't charge or reclaim the VAT on them. For example, out of scope items include:

Exempt goods and services

Exempt goods or services are supplies that you can't charge VAT on:

- must not be included in your VAT records.
- If you buy or sell an exempt item you should still record the transaction in your general business accounts.
- Examples of exempt items include:
- Insurance.
- postage stamps or services
- health services provided by doctors.

VAT registration

Businesses that sell only VAT-exempt goods and services can't register for VAT. If you start selling items that aren't exempt, you can register for VAT voluntarily.

You must register if the total value of non-exempt goods and services goes over the VAT taxable turnover threshold.

Circumstance	Threshold	What to Do
Total taxable turnover	Total taxable turnover	Register for VAT
Bringing Goods into Northern Ireland from the EU (Acquisitions)	More than £85,000	Register for VAT
Selling goods from Northern Ireland to consumers in the EU ('distance selling')	Total sales across the EU over £8,818	Register for VAT in EU countries
VAT registered - taxable turnover	Less than £83,000	Cancel VAT registration (optional)

There are other rules on reporting VAT if you sell goods from Northern Ireland to VAT-registered businesses in the EU.

Charging VAT to charities

As a VAT-registered business, you can sell certain goods and services to charities at the zero or reduced rate of VAT. It's your responsibility to check if the charity is eligible, and to apply the correct rate. Community amateur sports clubs (CASCs) don't qualify for VAT reliefs for charities. See Chapter 6 for more about giving to charities.

Free goods and services

You don't have to pay VAT on things like free samples if they meet certain conditions.

Providing services to EU businesses

If you supply services to a business customer in the EU, you don't need to charge VAT - the customer is responsible for paying VAT in their country. There are different rules for some services, like:

- hiring transport.
- land or property services (for example, valuing property, agricultural work or repairing a building)
- events.
- restaurant or catering services.
- physical services you do to someone else's goods like manufacturing, cleaning or making alterations.

- services where you act as an intermediary such as being a broker or agent.
- digital services.

****

Chapter 10

Business and Pension Provision

In this chapter, we look at pensions generally and the tax liabilities of saving for one's own personal pension (self-employed, partners and company directors) and the tax liabilities when contributing into employees' occupational schemes. We start with a summary of the different ways to save for a pension. For a fuller outline you should refer to A Straightforward Guide to Pensions and the Pensions Industry.

The State Pension
The State Pension system is based on contributions, the payments made by an individual today funds today's pension payments and for those who are young the future contributions will foot their pension bill. Therefore, the state pension system is not a savings scheme it is a pay-as-you-go system.

The full State Pension is £203.85 a week in the current 2023/24 tax year, or £10,600 a year, rising to £11,502 a year (£221.20 a week) in the 2024/25 tax year. The full old basic State Pension is £156.20 a week, and this will increase to £169.50 at the start of the new tax year. If you have fewer than 10 years of contributions, you won't receive any State Pension at all.

Occupational pensions

Occupational pension schemes are a very important source of income. With occupational pension schemes the contract is between the company and the pension provider. With Group Personal Pension Schemes,, although the employer chooses the company the contract is between the employee and the pension company.

Occupational pension schemes are one of the best ways to pay into a pension scheme as the employer has to contribute a significant amount to the pot. Over the years the amounts paid into occupational pension schemes has increased significantly. Although there have been several incidences of occupational schemes being wound up this is relatively small and they remain a key source of retirement income.

From October 2012, it has been compulsory for employers to provide an occupational pension scheme, Auto Enrolment. For the first time, employers are obliged to:

- enrol most of their workforce into a pension scheme; and
- make employer pension contributions.

This will affect all employers in the UK, regardless of the number of individuals that they employ. Anyone who is classed as a 'worker' for National Minimum Wage purposes is included in the new pension regime.

This was introduced in stages, and each employer was be given a 'staging date' determined by how many employees they had as of April 1st 2012. We will be discussing Auto Enrolment further in this chapter.

Private Pension Savings-General-The Lifetime allowance

There is a single lifetime limit on the amount of savings that a person can build up through various pension schemes and plans that are subject to tax relief. (This excludes the state pension). The lifetime allowance is £1,073,100 from April 2023. However, from April 2024, the government intends to scarp the allowance.

The lifetime allowance applies to savings in all types of pension schemes including occupational pensions and stakeholder schemes. There are, broadly, two types of scheme or plan:

- Defined contribution-with these types of schemes money goes in and is invested with the fund used to buy a pension. Basically, if the fund at retirement is £200,000 then £200,000 lifetime allowance has been used up
- Defined benefit-in this type of scheme, a person is promised a pension of a certain amount usually worked out based on salary before retirement and the

length of time that you have been in the scheme. The equation for working out lifetime benefit in this type of scheme is a little more complicated. The pension is first converted into a notional sum (the amount of money it is reckoned is needed to buy a pension of that size). The government sets out a factor that it says will be needed to make the conversion which it has said is 20. If the pension is £20,000 then this is calculated as £20,000 times £20,000 which is £400,000. Therefore £400,000 will be used up from the lifetime allowance.

The annual allowance

The annual allowance (amount that an individual can contribute to a pension) is £60,000 (April 2023/24). This is the amount that pension savings may increase each year whether through contributions paid in or to promised benefits. In addition, you can carry forward from three years previously. The annual allowance will not start in the year a person starts their pension or die. This gives a person scope to make large last-minute additions to their fund.

Limits to benefits and contributions

The present benefit and contribution limits have been scrapped. The only remaining restrictions are:
- Contributions-the maximum that can be paid in each year is either the amount equal to taxable earnings or £3,600 whichever is the greater.

- Tax free lump sum-at retirement a person can take up to one quarter of the value of the total pension fund as a tax free lump sum.

Not all dependant pensions will benefit from the tax exemption, however. Where the member dies before the age of 75 with either uncrystallised funds or a drawdown fund, if the beneficiary chooses to buy an annuity with the fund rather than go into drawdown, this will remain fully taxable.

Automatic enrolment

As stated above, from 2012, changes to pensions law affected all employers with at least one worker in the UK. Employer's need to:

- Automatically enrol certain workers into a pension scheme.
- Make contributions on their workers behalf.
- Register with the Pensions Regulator.
- Provide workers with information about the changes and how they will affect them.
- Workers who need to be automatically enrolled are called 'eligible jobholders'. An eligible jobholder is:
- Aged between 22 and the state pension age.
- Working, or ordinarily working in the UK.
- Earning above a certain amount (currently £10,000).

Basic rules for Auto-Enrolment for 2023/4

- You're only required to auto enrol **eligible jobholders**. You must pay contributions towards their pension savings. You must enrol eligible jobholders even if they say they don't want to join the Scheme.
- **Non-eligible jobholders** can ask to join the Scheme. If they ask, you must put them in and pay contributions towards their pension savings.
- Unless you have alternative pension arrangements for **entitled workers**, they can also ask to join the Scheme and you must put them in.

Type of employee	Eligible Jobholder	Non-Eligible Jobholder	Entitled worker
Age	**22-State Pension age**	16-74	16-74
Earns	£10,000+	£6,240-£10,000	Below £6,240
Auto enrolment status	Must be auto-enrolled	Can ask to join	Can ask to join
Employer contribution status	Employer contributions required	Employer contributions required	Employer contributions required under scheme rules

- You're only required to auto enrol **eligible jobholders**. You must pay contributions towards their pension savings. You must enrol eligible jobholders even if they say they don't want to join the Scheme.

- **Non-eligible jobholders** can ask to join the Scheme. If they ask, you must put them in and pay contributions towards their pension savings.
- Unless you have alternative pension arrangements for **entitled workers**, they can also ask to join the Scheme and you must put them in.

Calculating contributions

There are several ways you can calculate contributions for auto enrolment. There are statutory minimum contribution levels, but you can choose to set higher contribution levels if you want to.

Qualifying earnings

This is the minimum basis for calculating auto enrolment pension contributions. Qualifying earnings are all earnings between a lower and upper limit set by the government and reviewed each year. In 2023-2024 the lower limit is £6,240 and the upper limit is £50,270.

The minimum auto enrolment contribution to an employee's pension savings is 8% of qualifying earnings. Employers must pay at least 3% and the employee the remaining 5%.

Qualifying earnings include salary, wages, commission, bonuses, overtime, statutory sick pay and statutory parental leave pay (maternity, paternity and adoption pay).

Basic earnings

These include basic pay, holiday pay and statutory pay such as sick pay or parental leave pay. They don't include bonuses, commission, overtime and similar payments.

If you use basic earnings to calculate auto enrolment pension contributions, the minimum contribution to an employee's pension savings is 9%. Employers must pay at least 4% and the employee the remaining 5%.

Total earnings

These are all earnings including basic pay, holiday pay, sick pay, bonuses, commission, overtime and similar payments. If you use total earnings to calculate auto enrolment pension contributions, the minimum contribution to an employee's pension savings is 7%. Employers must pay at least 3% and the employee the remaining 4%.

See table overleaf.

Definition	Qualifying earnings	Basic earnings	Total earnings
Includes	All earnings between a lower and upper limit set by the government and reviewed each year.	Basic pay, holiday pay and statutory pay such as sick pay, but not bonuses, commission, overtime and similar payments.	All earnings including basic pay, holiday pay, sick pay, bonuses, commission, overtime and similar payments.
Total minimum contribution	8%	9%	7%
Employer	3%	4%	3%
Employee	5%	5%	4%

Choosing a pension scheme

Employers with an automatic enrolment duty will need to choose a pension scheme they can use for automatic enrolment. Information from the Pensions Regulator is available to help inform this decision. Employers might use an existing scheme or set up a new one with a pension provider. In addition, there is the National Employment Savings Trust (NEST). NEST is a pension scheme with the following characteristics:

- It has a public service obligation, meaning it must accept all employers who apply.

137

It has been established by government to ensure that employers, including those that employ low to medium earners, can access pension savings and comply with their automatic enrolment duties.

Whether the scheme an employer uses for automatic enrolment is new or not, it must meet certain specific set out in legislation.

The scheme cannot:
- Impose barriers, such as probationary periods or age limits for workers.
- Require staff to make an active choice to join or take other action, e.g. having to sign a form or provide extra information to the scheme themselves, either prior to joining or to retain active membership of the scheme.

Each pension scheme will have its own rules, but all employers will need to provide the scheme with certain information about the person who is automatically enrolled.

Opt-out

Workers who have been automatically enrolled have the right to opt out of the employer's pension scheme by effectively giving one month's notice. To opt out, workers must give notice via an 'opt out' notice to the employer. When employers receive a valid opt out notice within the 1-month with pension funds can be obtained from the government.

Pensions for the Self-Employed

If you're self-employed, saving into a pension can be a more difficult habit to develop than it is for people in employment. There is no-one to choose a pension scheme for you, no employer contributions and irregular income patterns which can all make saving difficult. But preparing for retirement is crucial for you too.

How best to save for retirement

There are around 4.5 million people in the UK who are self-employed, and this number is increasing. Yet the number of self-employed people saving into a pension has halved. One big attraction of being self-employed is you don't have a boss. But, in terms of pensions, this is a disadvantage.

Make the most of your pension pot

The earlier you start saving into a pension, the better. It gives you more time to contribute to your savings before retirement, more time to benefit from tax relief, and more time for your savings to grow. Starting early could more than double your pension pot:

(overleaf)

*Assuming savings grew at 5% a year and charges were 0.75% a year

You pay	Government pays	Start saving at age	Pension pot at 65
£100	£25	30	£70,000
£100	£25	40	£46,000
£100	£25	50	£25,000*

Self-employed: what kind of pension should I use?

Most self-employed people use a personal pension for their pension savings. With a personal pension you choose where you want your contributions to be invested from a range of funds offered by the provider. The provider will claim tax relief at the basic rate of tax on your behalf and add it to your pension savings. How much you get back depends on how much is paid in, how well your savings perform, and the level of charges you pay.

Self-employed people can also use NEST (National Employment Savings Trust) which is the workplace pension scheme created by the government for auto enrolment. It's run as a trust by the NEST Corporation which means there are no shareholders or owners and it's run for the benefit of its members. Although NEST is primarily for people who are employed, they also allow some self-employed people to save with them.

If you are not sure which scheme to save with it would be worth consulting a regulated financial adviser who will make a recommendation based on your specific needs and circumstances. The benefit of taking regulated financial advice is you're protected if the product you buy turns out to be unsuitable or in the unlikely event the provider goes bust. But mostly the benefit is a financial adviser can search the whole market for you and make a recommendation personal to you.

****

Chapter 11

Closing Down, Selling or passing on a Business

In this chapter, we will look at the tax implications of closing down, selling or passing your business to someone else.

1. Closing a business down

There are many reasons why a business closes down, not least because it is not successful, but also because of retirement and a host of other personal reasons. The procedure for closing down depends very much on whether your business is unincorporated, such as a sole trader or partnership) or whether it is a limited company. Closing down a business that is unincorporated is relatively straightforward but a limited company is rather more complex, particularly if it is insolvent, when it can only be closed down through formal liquidation.

Self-employed or partnership-unincorporated business
When you commenced self-employment there were three tax-related things that you had to do:
- You registered your business with HMRC and arranged to pay National Insurance.

- You set up a PAYE scheme for employees (if you had any)
- You registered for VAT (if appropriate)

The first move then is to notify the National Insurance Contributions Office (NICO) that you are no longer self employed and liable to pay Class 2 contributions. You need to cease any direct debits.

Income tax

You will need to notify HMRC that you are no longer self-employed and prepare your accounts to the cessation date. You can claim overlap relief against your final profits if your original accounting year end was any date other than 31st of March or 5th of April. It is important that you have sufficient resources to be able to pay your final income tax bills.

Allocating profits to tax years

As we have discussed previously, there are special rules in operation for taxing business profits when a business starts. The same is the case when a business closes. The way in which these rules operate depends very much on the date on which you cease to trade and your last accounting year-end. Sometimes there is an overlap if you have been self-employed for a short period. In this case you can claim overlap relief.

With Overlap relief, overlap profits would have been created when you commenced self-employment because you chose to prepare your accounts to a date other than March 31st or April 5th. You may have already used some of your overlap profits if you changed your year-end. Any overlap relief that is left over can be deducted from the taxable profits of your final self-employed year. You will have an idea how much your overlap profits are as each year you enter them in the self-employed section of your tax return.

Treatment of stock

When you cease to be self-employed, in all likelihood, unless you have planned otherwise, you will have left over stock. For tax purposes, it must be valued accurately. If you take it from the business for personal use, it must be valued at market price. If you sell it to someone who is connected to you personally, such as a spouse or civil partner, or a relative, it is valued at its sale price or cost whichever is the higher.

Treatment of capital allowances

You cannot claim writing down allowances or annual investment or first year allowances when closing down your business. It is also very likely that you will take some assets out of your business, such as a vehicle, when you cease trading. These assets must be taken out of the capital allowance calculation at their market value. The same rule applies if you sell the assets to someone connected to you. If you make a loss in your final year, it is treated in the same way.

Any income or expenses incurred after your business has ceased trading

After your business has ceased trading, you might receive income or incur expenditure related to your business. These are known as post-cessation receipts and are either treated as taxable income in the year you receive them or, if you receive the income within six years of closing the business you can ask for them to be treated as income of the year when you ceased trading.

The types of expenses that you can claim as post-cessation expenses are:
- The costs of remedying any defective works.
- Damages.
- Any associated legal and insurance costs.
- Any bad debts you may have incurred or and costs associated with the recovery of bad debts.
- Professional indemnity insurance.

PAYE scheme

You must inform HMRC that you will no longer run a PAYE scheme from the designated date.

VAT registration

If you are registered for VAT you will need to contact the VAT office and cancel your registration from the designated date. Again, ensure that you have enough money set aside to meet final bills.

Closing down a limited company

As we have mentioned, the tax implications of closing down a limited company are more complicated than the rules for self-employment or partnership. Just how complicated depends on whether the company is a going concern (solvent), in administration or liquidation.

Striking a company off the register of companies

This is the simplest way of getting rid of a limited company. However, you can only do this if you obtain HMRC approval. Consent will only usually be given if you have filed final accounts and all returns and settled any outstanding taxes, such as corporation tax, PAYE and VAT. You will need, if this is the case, to pay out any remaining profits as dividends before applying to strike the company off.

A capital gain could arise on the distribution of the final profits in the company but this depends on the original costs of the shares, the amount paid out and the availability of the annual exemption.

De-registering for VAT

When you cease your business, you have to deregister for VAT. You will have to file a final return on the cessation date. In your final return you may have to account for VAT on any unsold stock or assets such as equipment and vans (but not cars), computers, furniture and so on. You should value these items at the price that you would expect to pay for them in their present condition. If their value is such that you would pay less than £1,000 of VAT you do not have to account for VAT. If HMRC are satisfied with your application for deregistration you will receive official confirmation of deregistration on form VAT 35. From the date of deregistration you must not charge VAT. In some circumstances, you can reclaim VAT for up to three years after deregistration on:

- bad debts that are irrecoverable
- Professional invoices, provided that the services relate to the period when you were VAT registered.

For further detailed information on VAT deregistration you should go to: www.gov.uk/vat-registration/cancel-registration.

Closing down a PAYE scheme

As well as notifying HMRC of the cessation of your PAYE scheme there are other steps for you to take, bearing in mind your responsibilities under employment law. The most important areas are as follows:

- You will need to ensure that employees are paid up until their leaving date, including other payments due such as holiday pay.
- Issue employees with a P45 until you use Real Time Information.
- Pay any redundancy payment (see below)

- Complete all other necessary forms such as end of year returns.
- Finally, pay any any outstanding tax and national insurance related to PAYE.

Making staff redundant

If you are laying off staff because you are closing your business, it is important to remember that you are liable to pay them statutory redundancy pay if they have been employed by you for two or more years. If you are a director employed by the company, you may also be entitled to stautory redundancy. An employee will normally be entitled to statutory redundancy pay if they have been working for you for 2 years or more. They will get:

- 1.5 weeks' pay for each full year of employment after their 41st birthday.
- a week's pay for each full year of employment after their 22nd birthday.
- half a week's pay for each full year of employment up to their 22nd birthday.

The length of service is capped at 20 years.

If they were made redundant on or after 6 April 2021, their weekly pay is capped at £643 and the maximum statutory redundancy pay they can get is £16,320.

Redundancy payments are not liable to tax or national insurance, as are any unpaid wages. Should you decide to pay your employees an amount above the statutory minimum, they will not be liable to tax or National Insurance as long as the payment is £30,000 or less. For more detailed advice on rights and obligations in relation to redundancy go to www.gov.uk/redundancy.

2. Selling a business

Selling a business is complicated and for certain you will require professional help. You want to make sure that the price you receive for what you have built up is a fair valuation and reflection of what you have put in to make the business a viable concern. Like closing down a business, the tax consequences for sole traders and partners are relatively straightforward. For a company, they are more complex, as you can either sell the individual assets of the company or sell the entire company by selling its shares.

Sole traders

If you are self-employed, you cannot sell the 'business' as such because legally there is nothing to sell. You can, however, sell off the assets such as land and buildings and goodwill (this might include your list of customers). In certain situations, it might be worthwhile incorporating your self-employment in order to sell it. This means becoming a limited company. You will need professional advice if you want to do this. There are tax consequences of 'selling' a self-employed business, particularly the assets, as follows:

- Capital gains tax-land and buildings, plus any plant fixed to a building, goodwill and other intangible assets such as patents, licences, rights and designs (this list is not exhaustive) are all liable to capital gains tax. You must work out the gain on each item, deduct the original acquisition cost, and also purchase and sale costs and work out the gain. You also can claim any relief you might be entitled to, such as Business Asset Disposal relief (formerly Entrepreneurs Relief).
- Equipment on which you have claimed capital allowances is not liable to capital gains tax unless the selling price for an individual item is £6,000 or more. Chattels relief will reduce any gain that arises. The word 'chattel' is a legal term meaning an item of tangible, moveable property – something you can both touch and move. Your personal possessions will normally be chattels.
- Income from the sale of stock will be included in your final trading accounts and be liable to income tax.
- If you sell your debts then there is no capital gains tax to pay. If you receive less than the debts are worth then you can include a deduction for bad debts in your final trading accounts.

You may also be liable for VAT on some of the assets if you are not selling the business as a going concern.

Partners

A partnership may sell its assets or the individual partners may sell their share in the partnership. If a partnership sells its assets to a third party, the tax consequences are the same as they are for a sole trader, with each partner being liable for capital gains tax on their share. Commonly, one partner will sell to another. If this is the case, and the partnership continues, the withdrawal of your investment has no capital gains liability, unless the partnership assets are re-valued and you are given a share of that profit resulting from that re-valuation.

Limited company

When a company sells its business, as opposed to closing down, there will be two options:
- It can sell its assets or
- It can sell its shares.

The vendor of the business will usually prefer to sell shares because this minimises their capital gains liability. However, the buyer will usually prefer to buy assets because it is more straightforward and less risky than taking on all the company's liabilities.

Purchasing assets has the following tax advantages:
- Capital allowances can be claimed.
- A tax deduction can be claimed on the write-off of the goodwill (assuming that the purchaser is a company)
- Rollover relief may be claimed.

If the purchaser can be persuaded to buy shares instead, there are several tax advantages:

- Stamp duty on the acquisition of shares is less than the cost of stamp duty land tax on the purchase of land and buildings.
- There is no VAT on the sale of shares.
- In some circumstances, the vendor may wish to sell assets instead of shares where for example it has trading losses which can be offset against the gains and it can claim rollover relief.

VAT

VAT on the sale of a business is complex. If a business is sold as a going concern, you do not have to charge VAT on the sale. This presupposes that the buyer will take over and operate the business without any major changes. If the assets are sold, only VAT must be charged. Sometimes VAT can be charged on buildings even if the business is sold as a going concern. This area is complex and you will need to take advice as to what is the most tax efficient way to sell your business.

Cash or shares?

When you sell the company, you need to have in place an agreement as to what you will receive and when exactly you will receive it.

The straightforward option is for you to receive cash. Essentially, this means that, at the close of the transaction you receive payment. Your tax liability is calculated according to whether you have sold shares or assets. If you agree to sell your shares to another company there is an alternative to being paid in cash. You can trade your shares for shares in the purchasing company.

You have probably seen this in the financial news where one company takes over another. You can also exchange shares for loan stock. The advantage of this 'paper exchange, i.e. shares for shares or loan stock is that you do not pay capital gains tax until you eventually dispose of the shares.

Earn out

If as part of the sale agreement, you are having a continuing involvement in the business (this happens in many cases) then you may not get the full complement of shares straight away as some may be held back and transferred to you only if the company's performance meets expectations. This is termed 'earn out' and the value of the earn out is treated as part of the shares being exchanged, so no capital gains tax is due until the shares are sold.

Other important areas: There are other areas your accountant may want to discuss with you such as claiming Rollover Relief, the Enterprise Investment Scheme Deferral Relief and the SEED Enterprise Investment Scheme

One thing is very apparent and that is when you decide to sell a company you will require professional help from experienced advisors. They will assist in the following areas:

- Negotiation of the sale with the purchaser.
- Calculate tax liabilities.
- Suggest ways to minimise tax liabilities, including capital gains tax and VAT.
- On a share sale, provide the purchaser with financial information so that they can check out the company's liabilities. This is called 'due diligence'.
- On a share sale, negotiate with the purchaser regarding the indemnities and warranties they require concerning the company's tax liabilities.
- Draw up the sale document.
- Deal with any necessary conveyances and deal with stamp duty.
- Contact HMRC as and when necessary.

*3. Passing on a business-*Giving away your business

Many people, when they reach retiring age, or simply decide that they have had enough, decide to pass on their business. This is usually to family but it can also be to the next generation of managers. Such transactions have capital gains and inheritance tax implications, although there will be no immediate capital gains charge due to what is known as 'gift relief'. This is outlined below. Also, in relation to inheritance tax, you may be entitled to agricultural or business relief.

If you transfer your business to family, it has to be valued commercially because it is being transferred to a 'connected person'. If you give your business to your spouse or civil partner, the business is transferred for capital gains purposes at its cost, so there is no gain or loss so therefore no capital gains liability. For inheritance tax purposes the business is usually transferred to a spouse or civil partner at commercial value but there is no inheritance tax to pay if they are from the UK. If they are not from the UK, there is a ceiling on the amount that can be passed over.

Gifts relief

You may be able to claim Gift Hold-Over Relief if you give away business assets (including certain shares) or sell them for less than they are worth to help the buyer. Gift Hold-Over Relief means:

- you don't pay Capital Gains Tax when you give away the assets.
- the person you give them to pays Capital Gains tax (if any is due) when they sell (or 'dispose of') them.

Tax isn't usually payable on gifts to your husband, wife, civil partner or a charity.

Eligibility

The conditions for claiming relief depend on whether you're giving away business assets or shares.

If you're giving away business assets
You must:
- be a sole trader or business partner, or have at least 5% of shares and voting rights in a company (known as your 'personal company')
- use the assets in your business or personal company.

You can usually get partial relief if you used the assets only partly for your business.

If you're giving away shares
The shares must be in a company that's either:
- not listed on any recognised stock exchange.
- your personal company.

The company's main activities must be in trading (eg providing goods or services) rather than non-trading activities like investment.

Working out the relief
You don't pay Capital Gains Tax on any assets you give away. You might need to pay tax if you:
- sell an asset for less than it's worth to help the buyer.
- make a gain on what you paid for it.

How to claim
You must claim jointly with the person you give the gift to. Send your claim at the time you give them the gift. Fill in the

form in the relief for gifts and similar transactions helpsheet and include it with your Self Assessment tax return. If you send your tax return online, upload a scanned copy of the form. HM Revenue and Customs has more information on claiming Gift Hold-Over Relief if you're a trustee.

Inheritance tax
If you live for seven years or more after transferring your business, there will be no inheritance tax liability. This type of transfer, made during your lifetime, is called a 'potentially exempt transfer'. this means that the transfer is potentially but not absolutely exempt. If you die within seven years of making the transfer there may be inheritance tax to pay. If you are entitled to 100% business relief or agricultural property relief no inheritance tax will be charged on the potentially exempt transfer. However, this relief can be called into question if the person you give the property to disposes of it before you die or the property ceases to meet the conditions to qualify for the relief.

For more detailed information on inheritance tax liabilities and passing on a business go to www.gov.uk/business-relief-inheritance-tax/overview.

If you die-what happens to your business?
Not may people want or expect this but it can and does happen. It is vital that you make a will that takes into account tax planning. If you do not make a will then your business will

go to dependants in a given order of succession, according to the current laws of succession. things could get messy and tax liabilities mount, unless of course the situation is challenged and a variation achieved which can be complex and costly. Better to make a will and, as your business dealings become ever more complex, review it carefully every two years at least!

A good site for basic advice is:

https://www.gov.uk/selling-your-business-your-responsibilities/business-partnership

In addition, there are a number of very good sites that will advise you on preparing a business for sale. One such site is:

https://uk.businessesforsale.com/uk/sell

****

Useful addresses and websites

Association of Taxation Technicians
30 Monck Street
London
SW1P 2AP
Phone: +44 (0)20 7340 0551
email: info@att.org.uk
www.att.org.uk

Association of Certified Chartered Accounts (ACCA)
www.accaglobal.com

Institute of Chartered Accountants England and Wales
ICAEW
Chartered Accountants' Hall
1 Moorgate Place,
London
EC2R 6EA
www.icaew.com
01908 248 250

Institute Members Scotland
PO Box 26198
Dumfermline, KY12 8ZD
0131 1251

Chartered Accountants Ireland
Chartered Accountants House,
47-49 Pearse Street,
Dublin 2

Chartered Accountants House,
32-38 Linenhall Street,
Belfast,
County Antrim
BT2 8BG,
United Kingdom
www. charteredaccountants.i.e

Chartered Institute of Taxation
30 Monck Street
London SW1P 2AP
Phone: +44 (0)20 7340 0550
www.tax.org.uk

The Association of Accounting Technicians.
30 Churchill Place
London
EC14 5RE
www.aat.org.ukLondon E20 1JN

The Financial Conduct Authority
12 Endeavour Square

London E20 1JN
0300 500 8082
https://www.fca.org.uk/

Government Departments
HMRC
www.gov.uk/government/organisations/hm-revenue-customs

Inheritance tax
www.gov.uk/inheritance-tax

The Insolvency Service
www.gov.uk/government/organisations/insolvency-service

National Insurance
www.gov.uk/national-insurance/overview

Department for Work and Pensions
www.gov.uk/government/organisations/department-for-work-pensions

Pensions-The Pensions Regulator
www.thepensionsregulator.gov.uk

Auto-Enrolment
www.autoenrolment.co.uk

Department for Business, Energy and Industrial Strategy
https://www.gov.uk/government/organisations/department-for-business-energy-and-industrial-strategy

****

INDEX

Adoption pay, 8, 88
Agency workers, 93
Annual allowance, 132
Annual General Meetings, 32
Annual investment allowance, 6, 66
Auto Enrolment, 130, 131
Automatic enrolment, 10, 133
Autumn statement, 21

Business accounts, 15
Business Asset Disposal Relief (BADR), 112
Business Asset Rollover Relief, 115
Business cars, 6, 69
Business Premises, 9, 105
Business rates, 106

Capital assets, 17
Capital gains tax, 4, 35, 40, 112, 151
Cars, 41, 70, 71
Cash basis accounting, 3, 25
Chargeable assets, 41
Closing Down, 11, 143
Companies House, 16
Corporation tax, 35, 38

Defined benefit, 131
Defined contribution, 131
Direct taxes, 4, 35

Dividends, 39
Donating money, 7, 76

Enerprise Schemes, 41
Entrepreneurs relief, 9
Extraordinary General Meeting, 32

First year allowances, 6, 68, 70, 71, 72
Fixtures, 6, 65
Forming a company, 33

Giving to Charity, 7, 75

Her Majesty's Revenue and Customs, 29
HM Revenue and Customs, 16, 21, 23, 36, 92, 96, 97, 116, 120, 158
Home insurance policies, 105

Income tax, 4, 11, 35, 36, 37, 86, 144
Indirect taxes, 4, 36
Individual savings Accounts (ISA's, 37
Inheritance tax, 4, 12, 35, 43, 158, 163

Limited Company, 4, 14, 15, 32, 39
Limits to benefits and contributions, 10, 132

Machinery, 63
Mixed partnerships, 6, 67
National Insurance, 5, 17, 18, 22, 24, 35, 48, 49, 86, 87, 88, 89, 91, 93, 94, 95, 97, 143, 144, 150, 163

National Living Wage, 85

Occupational pensions, 10, 130
Overlap relief, 11, 144

Partnership, 14, 15, 30
Passing on a Home, 44
PAYE, 8, 11, 17, 18, 27, 31, 49, 85, 86, 89, 92, 93, 94, 144, 146, 147, 148, 149
Pensions, 10, 36, 129, 133, 137, 139, 163
Pensions Regulator, 133, 137
Perks, 9, 98
Plant, 63, 64
Premium bond income, 37
Pre-trading tax breaks, 17
Private Pension Savings-General, 10, 131
Profits, 31

Redundancy payments, 37, 149
Rollover relief, 9, 115, 152

SEED enterpise, 41
Self-assessment, 19
Self-employed, 8, 11, 89, 140, 143
Self-Employed, 139
Selling, 9, 11, 110, 143, 150
Shareholders, 31, 32
Sole Traders, 14
Sources of pension, 10, 129
State Pension, 10, 129

Statutory Paternity Leave, 87
Statutory Paternity Pay, 8, 86, 87, 88
Student loan repayments, 8, 96
Students, 8, 94

Tax credits, 37
Tax free lump sum, 133
Tax Liability for Businesses, 4, 35
The annual allowance, 10, 132
The lifetime allowance, 10, 131
The Minimum Wage, 85
The state pension, 129

Uncrystallised funds, 133
Utilities, 106

VAT rates, 10, 122
Volunteers, 8, 94

Appendix 1 National Insurance Classes and Rates

National Insurance contributions	Employee and employer Class 1 rates and thresholds (£ per week) 2024/5
Lower Earnings Limit (LEL)	£123
Primary Threshold (PT)	£242
Secondary Threshold (ST)	£175
Upper Earnings Limit (UEL)	£967
Upper Secondary Threshold for under 21s	£967
Apprentice Upper Secondary Threshold (AUST) for under 25s	£967
Freeport Upper Secondary Threshold (FUST)	£481
Investment Zones Upper Secondary Threshold (IZUST)	£481

Veteran Upper Secondary Threshold (VUST)	£967
Employment Allowance (per employer)	£5,000
Employee's (primary) Class 1 contribution rates (£ per week)	**2024/25**
Earnings band	
Below Lower Earnings Limit (LEL)	Not applicable
Lower Earning Limit (LEL) to Primary Threshold (PT)	0%
Primary Threshold (PT) to Upper Earnings Limit (UEL)	8%
Married Woman's reduced rate for (Primary) Class 1 contribution rates	**2024/25**
Weekly earnings from between the Primary Threshold (PT) and Upper Earnings Limit (UEL)	1.85%
Weekly earnings above the Upper Earnings Limit (UEL)	2%

Employer's (secondary) Class 1 contribution rates	**2024/25**
Below Secondary Threshold (ST)	0%
Above Secondary Threshold (ST)	13.8%
Employer's (secondary) Class 1 contribution rates for employees under 21	**2024/25**
Below Upper Secondary Threshold (UST)	0%
Above Upper Secondary Threshold (UST)	13.8%
Employer's (secondary) Class 1 contribution rates for Apprentices under 25	**2024/25**
Below Apprentice Upper Secondary Threshold (AUST)	0%
Above Apprentice Upper Secondary Threshold (AUST)	13.8%

Employer's (secondary) Class 1 contribution rates for eligible employees of Freeports	2024/25
Below Freeports Upper Secondary Threshold (FUST)	0%
Above Freeports Upper Secondary Threshold (FUST)	13.8%

Employer's (secondary) Class 1 contribution rates for eligible employees of Investment Zones	2024/25
Below Investment Zone Upper Secondary Threshold (IZUST)	0%
Above Investment Zone Upper Secondary Threshold (IZUST)	13.8%

Employer's (secondary) Class 1 contribution rates for qualifying veterans	2024/25
Below Veterans Upper Secondary	0%

Threshold (VUST)	
Above Veterans Upper Secondary Threshold (VUST)	13.8%

Self-employed Class 2 contributions rates and thresholds (£ per week) Class 2 thresholds (£ annual profit)	**2024/25**
Small Profits Thresholds (SPT)	£6,725
Lower Profits Thresholds (LPT)	N/A

Class 2 contribution rates (£ per week)	**2024/25**
Below Small Profits Threshold (SPT)	£3.45 (Voluntary)
Small Profits Threshold (SPT) to Lower Profits Threshold (LPT)	0%
Above Lower Profits Threshold (LPT)	0%
Special Class 2 rate for share fisherman	£4.10

Special Class 2 rate for volunteer development workers	£6.15
Class 3 National Insurance contributions: other rates and thresholds (£ per week)	**2024/25**
Voluntary contributions	£17.45
Self-employed Class 4 rates and thresholds (£ per year)	**2024/25**
Lower Profits Limit (LPL)	£12,570
Upper Profits Limit (UPL)	£50,270

The main and additional rates of Class 4 National Insurance contributions are assessed on an annual basis, therefore an average rate was applied to ensure consistency and fairness with Class 1 National Insurance contributions payers who paid the increased National Insurance contributions rate between 6 April and 5 November 2022.

Self-employed National Insurance contributions are calculated on an annual basis; therefore, the Lower Profits Limit was set at an average threshold of £11,908 for the 2022 to 2023 tax year which is equivalent

TAX FOR SMALL TO MEDIUM SIZE BUSINESS

to 13 weeks of the threshold at £9,880 and 39 weeks at £12,570, reflecting the position for employees.

Class 4 contribution rates	
Below Lower Profits Limit (LPL)	0%
Lower profits Limit (LPL) to Upper Profits Limit (UPL)	6%
Above Upper Profits Limit (UPL)	2%

The main and additional rates of Class 4 National Insurance Contributions are assessed on an annual basis, therefore an average rate was applied to ensure consistency and fairness with Class 1 National Insurance Contributions payers who paid the increased National Insurance Contributions rate between 6 April and 5 November 2022.

Self-employed National Insurance Contributions are calculated on an annual basis; therefore, the Lower Profits Limit was set at an average threshold of £11,908 for the 2022 to 2023 tax year which is equivalent to 13 weeks of the threshold at £9,880 and 39 weeks at £12,570, reflecting the position for employees.

****

www.straightforwardbooks.co.uk

All titles, listed below, in the Straightforward Guides Series, and further books in the Emerald Guides Series, can be purchased online by going to www.straightfowardbooks.co.uk

Law, Including Emerald Guides

Consumer Rights
Bankruptcy Insolvency and the Law
Employment Law
Healthcare Rights and law
Private Tenants Rights
Family law
Small Claims in the County Court
Contract law
Intellectual Property and the law
Divorce and the law
Leaseholders Rights
The Process of Conveyancing
Knowing Your Rights and Using the Courts
Producing Your own Will
Housing Rights
The Bailiff the law and You
Probate and The Law
Company law
What to Expect When You Go to Court
Give me Your Money-Guide to Effective Debt Collection
Being a Litigant in Person

Conveyancing Residential property
A Practical Guide to Obtaining Probate
Marriage and Same Sex Partnerships
A Guide to Powers of Attorney
Mental Health and the Law

General titles, Including Emerald Guides

Letting Property for Profit
Buying, Selling and Renting property
Bookkeeping and Accounts for Small Business
Creative Writing
Freelance Writing
Writing Your own Life Story
Writing performance Poetry
Writing Romantic Fiction
Speech Writing
The Straightforward Business Plan
The Straightforward C.V.
Successful Public Speaking
Handling Bereavement
Individual and Personal Finance
The Crime Writers casebook
Being a Detective
A Comprehensive Guide to Arrest and Detention
A Comprehensive Guide to Burglary and Robbery
The Bailiff and You
Beating The Bully
Explaining Autism

Explaining Diabetes
Explaining Alzheimer's and Dementia
Explaining Asthma
Stop Smoking Now
Mind Power and Healthy Eating

Go to:

www.straightforwardbooks.co.uk